COLLECTOR'S COMPASS™

20th Century
Dinnerware

Martingale™
& C O M P A N Y

Credits

President . . . . Nancy J. Martin
CEO . . . . Daniel J. Martin
Publisher . . . . Jane Hamada
Editorial Director . . . . Mary V. Green
Editorial Project Manager . . . . .Tina Cook
Series Editor . . . . Christopher J. Kuppig
Copy Editor . . . . Allison A. Merrill
Design and Production Manager . . . . Stan Green
Cover and Studio Photographer . . . . Brent Kane
Series Designer . . . . Bonnie Mather
Production Designer . . . . Jennifer LaRock Shontz
Series Concept . . . . Michael O. Campbell

Martingale™ & COMPANY

Collector's Compass™: 20th Century Dinnerware
© 2001 by Martingale & Company

Martingale & Company
20205 144th Avenue NE
Woodinville, WA 98072-8478 USA
www.martingale-pub.com

Printed in Canada
06 05 04 03 02 01   8 7 6 5 4 3 2 1

On the cover: Fiesta disk pitchers, in cobalt (water) and yellow (juice).

Library of Congress Cataloging-in-Publication Data
20th century dinnerware.
        p. cm. — (Collector's compass)
    Includes bibliographical references and index.
    ISBN 1-56477-377-9
    1. Tableware—Collectors and collecting—United States. I. Title: Twentieth
century dinnerware. II. Title: XXth century dinnerware. III. Series.

NK8725 .A15 2001
738.3'09'04075—dc21   2001016246

Mission Statement
We are dedicated to providing quality products and service by working
together to inspire creativity and to enrich the lives we touch.

CONTENTS

FOREWORD

As America's favorite hobby, collecting is exciting, gratifying, and above all, fun—but without the right knowledge, you could be destined for disappointment. Luckily, you've just found the most resourceful and inspiring series of guidebooks available to help you learn more about collecting. The Collector's Compass series approaches collecting in a whole new way, making it easy to learn about your favorite collectible categories—from the basics to the best-kept secrets.

The International Society of Appraisers (ISA) is pleased to be associated with the Collector's Compass series. As the ISA celebrates twenty years of professional education and certification of personal-property appraisers, who currently specialize in more than two hundred areas of expertise, we remain committed to setting the highest standards for our accredited members. The Collector's Compass series of reference books reflects the ISA's dedication to quality and integrity.

Christian Coleman, ISA CAPP, Retired
Executive Director, International Society of Appraisers

*I*NTRODUCTION

Whether it means setting the alarm clock for Saturday morning yard sales, watching *Antiques Roadshow,* or chasing down childhood memories on eBay, collecting has become America's favorite hobby. The joy of finding treasure amid the clutter of a tag sale or a screen full of online offerings is infectious. Who could resist a pastime that combines the fun of shopping, the thrill of the hunt, the lure of a bargain, and the pride of ownership?

Throngs of novice collectors are joining experienced veterans in online bidding and weekend antiquing expeditions. If you count yourself among them, this book is for you.

The editors of the Collector's Compass series realized that today's collectors need more information than what was then obtainable, in an accessible and convenient format. Going beyond available price and identification guides, each Collector's Compass book introduces the history behind a particular collectible, the fascinating aspects that make it special, and exclusive tips on where and how to search for exciting pieces.

Furthermore, the Collector's Compass series is uniquely reliable. Each volume is created by a carefully chosen team of dealers, appraisers, collectors, and other experts. Their collaboration ensures that each title will contain accurate and current information, as well as the secrets they've learned in a lifetime of collecting.

We hope that in the Collector's Compass series we have addressed every area essential to building a collection. Whether you're a newcomer or an experienced collector, we're sure this series will lead you to new treasures. Enjoy the adventure!

Moby Dick 12" chop plate, designed by Rockwell Kent for the Famous Artists series and produced by Vernon Kilns. *Photo courtesy of Star Center Mall.*

THE DRAWING POWER OF DISHES

What attracts collectors to the humble plate or cup and saucer? Perhaps it's the recognition of the familiar, the appeal of something you relate to over and over, day to day. Maybe it's a set of shapes, colors, or decorative patterns that just oozes the feel of your favorite design period. Or it could be the memories that dishes can conjure up of pleasant meals past, of family—of home.

Dinnerware—the everyday stuff, not special-occasion china—is one of the most popular and appealing collectibles in America. It's widely available, much of it is easily affordable, and you can use it. Whether you're captivated by the beauty of hand-painted Blue Ridge or the stunning shapes of such modern designers as Russel Wright and Eva Zeisel, there is no shortage of reasons to love dishes. What other collectible offers such variety, along with the opportunity to express your personal style?

If you're not drawn to recapturing childhood memories, you may be interested in creating family traditions of your own. Or you may be attracted to the workmanship evident in pottery, or because a particular shape or pattern catches your eye. Perhaps collecting dinnerware fits with your interest in home decorating. Superb artisanship, quality of materials, and innovative designs make dinnerware particularly compelling. Whatever the attraction that leads you to collect American dinnerware, you have plenty of company.

Dinnerware collectors are fairly evenly split between men and women, usually age thirty and older. It's not unusual for people to begin collecting when they first establish a household. Most will continue to collect for a lifetime.

Some excellent collections are small, narrowly defined by their owners, and feature only unusual, experimental, or otherwise outstanding examples. But most people find that their collections grow and grow, limited only by space and financial resources. Dinnerware is easy to display on shelves or in cabinets, and because it was designed for everyday use it doesn't demand the delicate handling required of, say, fine glassware. A couple in East Liverpool, Ohio, boasts a massive ten-thousand-plus-piece collection of Harker pottery. It has taken over every room in their house!

White Clover creamer, salt, and pepper, designed by Russel Wright for Harker Pottery, pattern introduced in 1951. Although not a commercial success—it was in production for only four years—White Clover won a design award from the Museum of Modern Art. Collectors can find the pattern in four colors: charcoal, coral sand, golden spice, and meadow green. *Photo courtesy of Retrospective Modern Design.*

Another collector keeps more than fifteen thousand pieces of colorware—dishes such as Fiesta by Homer Laughlin and Ringware by Bauer, made in a palette of colors to be mixed and matched—in special rooms containing dozens of shelving units. His house resembles a museum storeroom. While few of us will amass collections that extensive, you'll probably want your dishes out where you can see them, use them, and share them with others.

Planning a Collection

There are as many ways to plan and organize a collection as there are collectors. Probably the most common is to collect sets by pattern. But many people who begin this way eventually branch out, eager to collect other pottery by the same designer, or all the sugar bowls or soup tureens made by a favorite pottery, or . . . Whatever organizing principle you can imagine, someone likely has such a collection.

By Pattern

Most collectors start out with the basics: plates, bowls, cups, and saucers. Then they "graduate" into the harder-to-find, more expensive serving shapes, such as platters, cake stands, and covered casseroles.

Even after you've selected the pattern, there are other choices to be made. You may have to decide which color combinations to collect and which to leave behind. Many patterns with decals or hand-painted designs have different motifs on each piece. Royal China's Currier and Ives is a pattern that everybody has seen if they've spent any time antiquing. This pattern, most popular in blue-and-white but also available in pink and green, keeps the interest of the collector because of the variety of motifs it features.

The most popular, in-demand lines, such as Fiesta and Ringware, have risen sharply in price. If you begin today to buy an avidly collected pattern, it will be expensive and difficult to amass a large collection. For example, Taylor Smith and Taylor's Lu-Ray and Hall China Company's Autumn Leaf were once reasonably priced, but the more exotic items from these lines have skyrocketed. Fortunately, a number of patterns, designers, and companies remain under-collected or relatively undiscovered.

By Designer

Many important designers were associated with single potteries, including Frederick Hurten Rhead and Don Schreckengost from Homer Laughlin and Victor Schreckengost from Salem China. But the ones most in demand today are known first for their shapes and second for the potteries that manufactured them.

These designers, including Russel Wright, Eva Zeisel, and Ben Seibel, were hotly sought after in their day by competing companies. Wright designed dishes for top Ohio potteries, such as Steubenville and Sterling, as well as for Iroquois in New York, and even helped to create the popular postwar Melmac lines. Hall China and Red Wing enlisted the design genius of Eva Zeisel. She created the successful Hallcraft Tomorrow's Classic design and the highly successful Red Wing Town and Country pattern. Even Roseville got in on the designer craze by bringing Ben Seibel on board in 1952 to design Raymor, the company's only dinnerware service.

By Manufacturer

Collections based on a single pottery company are extremely popular. There are large groups of collectors who will collect anything and everything made by their favorite manufacturer. Because many potteries had very long life spans, this can produce interesting and diverse collections.

Pottery-specific collectors often become overwhelmed by sheer quantity. Some narrow their search to a few shapes or lines, others to a certain group of decals or to dishes made during a limited period.

By Theme

Collecting by theme is a relatively recent development. The Mexican-theme decals used by Homer Laughlin, W. S. George, and Knowles, Taylor & Knowles all command high prices. People also try to get as many different shapes as possible decorated with petit-point decals (see facing page), used by almost every pottery during the '30s and '40s. Other collectors go for hand-painted decorations, from Southern Potteries' Blue Ridge to Stetson's lines.

By Form or Shape

There have always been collectors searching for different styles of cups and saucers, creamers (a very easy and inexpensive shape to collect), or salt and pepper shakers. Cookie jars and teapots are also perennial favorites.

Collecting by form can be an endless pursuit. You will never track down every example, but you will find treasures everywhere. Most collectors narrow their focus to keep the collection under control. But sometimes that will rule out the most wonderful finds. If you're collecting McCoy cookie jars, can you really stop yourself when you see a Brayton Laguna jar worth $500 sitting on the shelf of an antiques store for $65? Probably not, which may be why so many collectors eventually become dealers.

Petit-Point Decoration

This Eggshell Nautilus dinner plate from Homer Laughlin, with petit-point decal, is one of the many "needlework" designs that appeared on dinnerware in the 1930s. The Nautilus shape, which features shells embossed on handles, feet, and finials, was introduced in 1936. It was available as a full service or in combination with Fiesta (also introduced in 1936) as the Fiesta Harmony service. In 1937 Homer Laughlin launched an experimental lightweight ware called Eggshell on the Nautilus shape. Eggshell Nautilus was followed by Eggshell Swing and Eggshell Theme in 1938, and Eggshell Georgian in 1940. The series was continued successfully through the 1950s, and Nautilus was perhaps the most popular. *Photo courtesy of Home Grown Antiques.*

By Series

There are some collectors who concentrate on special series, such as calendar plates, state plates (Vernon Kilns has a particularly popular series), face plates (featuring, for example, George Washington), or advertising plates. These are usually people who collect anything related to their specific interest and don't consider themselves dinnerware collectors. However, cross-collectors sometimes become true believers.

Picture map of
Washington plate
by Vernon Kilns

Where to Find Dinnerware in the Marketplace

Many collectors get started at an antiques-and-collectibles mall or local antiques shop—good venues for the novice. But if you want your collection to grow, you'll expand your shopping range. "Before You Begin Buying Dinnerware" on pages 47–64 provides an in-depth guide to buying in various venues, but here's a quick tour of the secondary market.

Yard and Garage Sales

The ever-popular yard or garage sale is the place to "get down and dirty." When you're digging through boxes of dishes wrapped in twenty-year-old newspapers, there's a thrill that can't be duplicated. Prices aren't always nickel-and-dime anymore, but you never know where the next bargain is hiding.

Always inspect merchandise carefully before you buy. No one is likely to refund your money when you discover that the lid on the teapot you just paid $50 for has been damaged and glued.

Thrift and Consignment Shops

Don't forget to visit the thrift stores in your area. Such charity organizations as the Salvation Army and Goodwill put out new things every day. Be prepared to see lots of chipped stuff, but keep looking because the next plate you pick up may be a Shawnee Corn-King, worth $40 to $50.

Consignment shops will generally be more expensive and won't carry obviously damaged dishes. Consignors are more likely to know the value of dinnerware than folks donating the contents of their basements to the thrift shop.

Auctions and Estate Sales

At auctions and estate sales you'll be in direct competition with dealers, but you don't have to mark up your purchases to make a living, so you can find great bargains. Always take advantage of the preview to examine closely any dishes you might bid on. Decide in advance how much you'll bid and stick to that figure.

Antiques Shops

Nothing beats spending a lazy Saturday browsing your local antiques stores. The atmosphere is much more civilized than at yard or estate sales. This is the best place for novices to learn from specialized dealers, too. Ask questions: most dealers will gladly share their knowledge. If you find a good dealer who offers quality merchandise, great service, and guaranteed satisfaction, patronize his or her shop regularly.

Dinnerware is such a huge category that few antiques dealers will be expert in every facet. So, contrary to popular wisdom, there are bargains to be found in antiques shops. That's one of the main reasons it really pays to make yourself the expert in what you collect.

Antiques-and-Collectibles Shows

At antiques-and-collectibles shows the merchandise is pricey, but you'll see the best examples in the best condition. Dealers save their premier pieces for these shows, and they're a terrific way to sample the incredible variety of dinnerware patterns and designs all in one place.

Internet Auctions

Branching out onto the Internet is a popular and efficient way to locate the piece you've been dying to add to your collection. There's simply no end to what's available. However, when several people are vying for a hard-to-find vintage Fiesta demi-pot (after-dinner coffeepot), competition can be fierce and big spenders will often steal away your prize at the last minute.

The Internet is making it easier to find pieces that were once considered rare. One collector reports, "During fifteen years of collecting Fiesta, I saw only three covered onion soups—considered by many collectors to be extremely difficult to find. Once I got online and on eBay, I started seeing them all the time!"

Dealers' Web Sites

More and more dealers are selling online, and the quality of merchandise is usually quite high. Chances are, you'll be working with a knowledgeable and reputable dealer who has a vested interest in building a good reputation and keeping repeat customers. On a dealer's site, unlike an online auction, there are set prices, but that doesn't mean you can't try to negotiate, or ask for free shipping.

Replacement Services

Dinnerware as a category—along with stemware and flatware—is unusual in that there are professional services which stock and sell most patterns. Collectors will sometimes canvass these replacement services for particularly difficult-to-find pieces, but prefer cheaper sources for everything else.

If you're looking for a dinner plate in a common Franciscan pattern, you're likely to find it in an antiques store for $10 to $15. Why would you pay $35 to a replacement service? On the other hand, if the service has the rare egg cup you've been searching everywhere for, you'll probably be happy to pay—whatever the cost.

Trade Papers

The Antique Trader Weekly, The Daze, and other trade papers are good sources of information on trends, shows, and auctions. Most issues are chock-full of classifieds, and many collectors like to buy this way. It's a bit risky for beginners: if you don't ask all the right questions, especially regarding condition, you might get stuck with something you don't want.

State of the Hobby

Collecting dinnerware has been popular for decades, but only recently have collectors shown such great enthusiasm and purchasing fervor. The economy has been strong, collecting is trendy, and people can indulge their nostalgia while they appreciate good design. Dinnerware, in short, is the perfect collectible.

The golden age of American potteries ended in the 1960s, when popular (and cheap) dinnerware imported from Japan was introduced to the market. Now the dinnerware category is in the "mature" phase of its development as a collectible. Though there are patterns yet to be discovered by collectors, for the most part the market is well established. Many of dinnerware's devotees have

Pebbleford eggcups by Taylor Smith and Taylor. Pebbleford was a common dinnerware in a coupe shape; the eggcups are rare. *Photo courtesy of Retrospective Modern Design.*

Extravagant Necessity?

Bauer Ringware is among the most expensive sets to collect. Some glaze colors in the pattern are especially dear: a 10½" white dinner plate has been known to sell for as much as $135 to $150. But this price pales in comparison with that fetched by the Fiesta covered onion soup, which sells in most colors for around $600. And because this shape was discontinued around the time turquoise was introduced, the extremely rare Fiesta turquoise covered onion soup has sold for as much as $10,000.

---

admired and collected for some time, yet the category is constantly attracting new collectors as young people discover that the quality and period charm of old-time dishes beat those of today's merchandise hands down.

Cross-category collectors also buy dinnerware, affecting supplies and pricing. Collectors of Hopalong Cassidy memorabilia, for instance, will search for the children's dinnerware sets made by W. S. George. Advertising pieces are popular crossover collectibles as well. Prices increase whenever there is more than one group of collectors searching for the same item.

A preponderance of active dealers, collectors, and observers believe that dinnerware shows all the signs of a healthy and growing hobby, including:

1. *New collectors.* As young adults establish homes of their own, new collectors are born.

2. *Number of publications.* More books and other publications about American dinnerware, and specific manufacturers and designers, are available than ever before.

3. *Collectors' clubs and associations.* Clubs devoted to the production of a single pottery, such as Frankoma, Red Wing, Stangl, and Watt, are proliferating. There are even clubs devoted to individual patterns, such as the National Autumn Leaf Collector's Society. And that's not all: you'll find collecting societies for cookie jars, salt-and-pepper sets, and other specific items.

4. *Web traffic and sales.* Check out the number of dinnerware items on eBay on any given day. Or research Web sites that sell

your particular pattern. You'll be surprised at the amount of traffic and information available.

5. *Sales of rare items.* Rare items are going for top dollar, which means that large numbers of advanced collectors are searching for limited-production items. Today, collectors will go to great lengths to find missing pieces, and they don't hesitate to pay whatever it takes.

Red Wing Potteries' varied output has earned the manufacturer a loyal following among collectors. Shown here is a Red Wing bread plate in the Magnolia pattern.

Value Trends

In general, prices for dinnerware are going up. As lesser-known lines become better known, values start to rise. There are two reasons. First, when an authoritative book comes out showcasing a specific shape or treatment, collectors often feel more comfortable in seeking it out. When there is very little information on a line, there tends to be very little interest. The second factor that forces prices up, even for undiscovered or under-collected lines, is the price of well-known lines. Sellers who have "old" dishes of any kind may presume they're valuable because they've seen the high prices associated with a very desirable line. And although dinnerware has been appreciated and collected for generations, when an entertainment guru such as Martha Stewart showcases a designer or pattern, suddenly it can be as though it just hit the market.

Older does *not* automatically equal more valuable. The number of collectors, rather than aesthetics or intrinsic value, drives prices. Some seventy-year-old sets of dishes in perfect condition have almost no value at all in today's marketplace, while a twenty-year-old piece of Pfaltzgraff in the recently discontinued Yorktowne pattern may sell for $30 or $40, even with a chip or two.

Modern designs have enjoyed a substantial increase in value during the past five to ten years. Whenever a design suddenly becomes popular, it typically first shows a dramatic rise in value, and then a slower, steady increase. Some of Ben Seibel's designs, including Harvest Time and Bridal White, both by Iroquois China Company, have increased in value by 25 to 50 percent per year during the past five years. Today, some of his designs remain undervalued, and the collector can expect prices for them to increase.

There are "standard" prices in the dinnerware market for most common patterns. For your initial purchases, consult the published sources and stay within those "book" price ranges. After you've shopped in a number of different venues, attended a few antiques shows, and learned everything you can about your collectible from publications and other collectors, you'll trust your own judgment when it comes to prices. Over time, the pieces you pay more than book value for will offset those you nab at bargain prices. Even more important than price, however, is condition: be cautious when you inspect merchandise for damage. If you pay too much for a piece in excellent condition, you may get your money back should you resell it; if you pay too much for a damaged piece, you'll never recoup your investment.

The dinnerware category least likely to hold its value is reproductions or reissues of American originals. For example, Johnson Brothers of England purchased the molds for Franciscan's Apple and Desert Rose patterns. Johnson produced many pieces from the original lines, some of which were quite rare. Today, pieces and sets of the patterns are available in many department stores and through some catalogs, such as J. C. Penney's. Reissued pieces are usually marked, so you won't unknowingly buy a new piece. While the reissue makes an attractive set, and is more affordable than the original hand-painted Franciscan dinnerware, it is not likely ever to be as valuable.

The value of most collections will appreciate over time, unless the dishes become overly worn and lose their glaze. Even under these circumstances, most collectors won't care, because they've enjoyed using their dishes over those many years. Of course, you'll want to care properly for your collection and maintain its value if possible, but all the experts agree that you should *collect what you love, use and enjoy it,* and not obsess about what it's worth.

Vintage Franciscan Desert Rose teacup and saucer, pattern introduced in 1941. *Photo courtesy of Star Center Mall.*

The Pfaltzgraff Village pattern—represented here by a utensil holder, coffeepot, and quiche dish—is a sort of tan-and-brown sequel to Yorktowne's blue and gray (see page 70). The two patterns are similar in their pieces and prices, though Yorktowne enjoys a little more cachet than Village, which was introduced around 1970 and continued in production until the late 1990s. Pfaltzgraff was one of the few American dinnerware manufacturers to survive the onslaught of importers in the 1960s. *Photo courtesy of Home Grown Antiques.*

ESSENTIAL BACKGROUND FOR DINNERWARE COLLECTORS

The first American potteries, established in Virginia about 1650, made earthenware crocks and pots. As early as the 1670s, a few companies in Pennsylvania, New York, and Massachusetts started to produce whiteware. Norton Pottery opened in Bennington, Vermont, in 1783 and produced a variety of earthenware and stoneware items. Tucker China began operations in 1825 in Philadelphia, and is believed to have been the first commercial porcelain manufacturer on this side of the Atlantic.

American dinnerware as we know it today is generally considered to have gotten its start in East Liverpool, Ohio, in the 1870s. Before that, such companies as Edwin Bennett, Harker, and Knowles, Taylor & Knowles were producing mostly utilitarian yellowware and Rockingham, a brown manganese-glazed earthenware. Greensboro Pottery and Pfaltzgraff Pottery, both in Pennsylvania, were making redware and other stoneware as early as 1810. Most of the early companies making everyday ware for food preparation, serving, and storage have vanished into history. Redware, yellowware, and brownware could not rival the china that was being imported, mostly from England.

By the mid-1800s there was a definite need to manufacture

whiteware in America. Potteries in the Ohio River Valley had an abundance of rich river deposits of clay, plenty of water, and a tradition of pottery making. New plants were built to handle the production of whiteware, and it rapidly became popular. The Homer Laughlin China Company won an award for its whiteware in 1876, and after 1890 began using the backstamp of an eagle atop the stomach of a lion—a mark signifying the end of British domination of the industry. Thus began the golden era of American dinnerware.

Americans were drawn to a more informal table for both lifestyle and financial reasons, and many important potteries did a wonderful job of marketing to this receptive audience. Dinnerware lines around the turn of the twentieth century often had as many as seventy-five pieces. By the 1930s, the number of items in sets had been reduced, to offer a more manageable table.

Blue Ridge Daisy bowl by Southern Potteries

The heyday of American dinnerware extended from about 1930 until the 1960s—a brief period when you consider that dishes have been continuously made and used throughout the last 350 years of our country's history. For some time after American products supplanted English ones in the late 1890s, our homegrown manufacturers were still deeply indebted to British design. It was not until the advent of Homer Laughlin's Fiesta, Bauer's Ringware, and Southern Potteries' hand-painted Blue Ridge patterns in the 1930s that American dishes started to establish their own identity. This led to an explosion of creativity that has rarely been matched in any field, culminating in the experimental work of designers Russel Wright, Eva Zeisel, and Frank Irwin, to name just a few.

In the '60s and '70s, dishes imported from Japan had a huge impact on the manufacture of American dinnerware. Many companies couldn't compete. Some closed, others merged or were bought out—only a handful survived. The desire of the American family for a more casual approach to dining didn't help sales of hand-decorated wares. People just weren't interested in buying expensive serving pieces from open stock.

Is all collectible dinnerware made of earthenware?

Generally, when we talk about collectible dinnerware we are referring to dishes made of clay. Earthenware dominates, but china and stoneware are also collectible. Of course, there is no reason why modern dinnerware can't be thought of more expansively. In the postwar years, plastics became the rage and certainly had an impact on the dinnerware market. Melmac and other types of plastic dinnerware became the everyday dishes for many Americans, and helped put many potteries out of business.

There have also been many manufacturers producing elaborate sets of glass dinnerware through the years. The twentieth century saw such popular variations as "Elegant" glass, Depression glass, and Fire King glass, all collectible in their own right. Despite these qualifications, it is safe to say that when collectors talk about dinnerware, they are usually referring to the clay-based pieces made by Homer Laughlin, Gladding McBean, Steubenville, and other potteries.

Lei Lani 7½" plate and 6" lug chowder bowl designed by Don Blanding for Vernon Kilns, pattern introduced in 1938. *Photo courtesy of Retrospective Modern Design.*

Were individual lines advertised to the public?

Indeed they were. And if the advertisements reflected real life, you would conclude that the world didn't exist outside your kitchen and the dishes you used. Prices were amazingly low, and merchandise was often guaranteed.

Advertising copywriters always know how to bring out the best in the worst of times. Part of one Fiesta ad from the 1930s read:

> Originating in California, inspired by colorful festivals of Mexico, Fiesta dinnerware has flashed across the country in a gay blaze of color. Its beautiful rainbow shades have captivated the hearts of housewives, bringing cheer and gaiety into the home, adding festive charm to Al Fresco dining.

This kind of advertising reads today as a denial of the hard times of the Great Depression, as if setting your table with these dishes could somehow transport you far away from thoughts of economic woe.

In the 1950s, Metlox advertised its Happy Time pattern of Provincial dinnerware in equally glowing terms. A brochure that accompanied sets of Happy Time read:

> This gay peasant pattern was created by famed Gisella under the art direction of Allen and Shaw. Hand painted under glaze for a lifetime of pleasant use, in charming outdoor-sy colors.

How was dinnerware originally purchased?

Dinnerware was shipped to retailers by the trainload to be sold in sets or as open stock. Some retailers gave manufacturers' stock patterns their own names. It's not unusual to find the same or similar patterns going by a number of different names in today's marketplace, depending on what retailer they were produced for.

Many people bought their dishes in luncheon or dinner "starter sets," boxed services for four. The buyer then selected the serving pieces desired from open stock. This encouraged the consumer to keep purchasing additional items.

How durable is my dinnerware? Will my investment last?

There's no single answer. Some wares are hardy, capable of withstanding lots of use and abuse before they crack, chip, or fade. Others are far more fragile and should be used only occasionally if their condition is to be preserved. You'll need to do some research to determine how the pattern or pottery you collect will hold up over time.

As a general guideline, Metlox, Gladding McBean's Franciscan, and Bauer consistently produced dinnerware of outstanding quality. Universal's Calico Fruit decal will fade rapidly if not cared for properly. But Hull's Mirror Brown can take all kinds of abuse and still look great. All of Pfaltzgraff's patterns have proved to be durable.

While every pottery had peaks and valleys, sometimes due to experimentation with clay bodies and glazes, high-quality American dinnerware was made to be durable and functional, and it generally is. To protect your investment, inspect merchandise carefully before you buy: telltale signs of a previous owner's hard wear or abuse will be evident under close examination (see "Now that You're Ready to Start Collecting" on pages 81–97).

A Mirror Brown or "brown drip" duck casserole (rare) and gravy boat with liner by Hull Pottery, pattern distributed from 1960 until the company went out of business, in 1985. Mirror Brown was one of the most popular lines of American dinnerware ever made, and the duck casserole is an inventive piece that's both functional and fun. *Photo courtesy of Home Grown Antiques.*

Is it safe to eat from my vintage dinnerware?

Almost all dinnerware made before the early 1970s, solid-color or otherwise, contains lead in the glaze. In the early '70s, the FDA tested dinnerware to determine if the lead leached into food placed on it, posing a risk of poisoning. In 1972, American potteries were required to stop using lead in their glazes.

Lead becomes a problem when vintage dinnerware containing certain acidic foods or liquids, such as tomato sauce, lemon juice, or vinegar, is heated in a microwave or conventional oven. Also, dishes that are heavily crazed should not be used when acidic foods will be held in them for an extended period. You can safely serve acidic foods on your vintage dinnerware; just remember not to heat or store such foods in them.

You'll also hear a lot of concerns about red glazes. Over hundreds of years, potteries have tried different glaze ingredients to achieve the color red. In fact, there is an ancient Chinese legend that illustrates just how difficult it is: An emperor commanded his chief potter to make earthenware with a bright, true-red glaze. After failing to produce the desired color, the despairing potter threw himself into the kiln. After the kiln cooled, everyone was astonished to see pots in a true red!

Red glazes generally contain traces of uranium oxide and must be fired at temperatures lower than those usual for earthenware (if the kiln is too hot, the red color "burns away," leaving an uneven brown). Are red glazes of concern today? Not really. Dozens of writers on Homer Laughlin's Fiesta red and other red-glazed ware have researched the scientific tests, and have determined that there is no real risk in eating from dishes with a red glaze if the glaze is uncompromised. Again, do not heat or store acidic foods on red-glazed dishes, especially if they are crazed.

When did dinnerware become collectible?

Generally speaking, items may become collectible either while still being sold in the primary market, or long after manufacture has been discontinued. In the case of most of the lines of American dinnerware collected today, the lines have become collectible many years after the dishes ceased being offered on the retail market.

Dinnerware introduced during the period from the 1920s through the 1950s didn't become collectible until the mid-1980s. In 1970, the tenth edition of one of the major collector books, *Warman's Antiques and Their Current Prices,* listed dozens of art potteries—such as Rookwood, Weller, and Roseville—as well as foreign dinnerware makers—Spode, Haviland, Meissen, Wedgwood—in abundance. Only a few U.S. dinnerware makers, such as Bennington and Tucker China, were included.

In the mid-1980s, American dinnerware came into its own. Hall China's famous Autumn Leaf, Harker's Cameoware, and Taylor Smith and Taylor's Lu-Ray were recognized as valuable and collectible. As more lines became collectible, books were devoted to covering these famous patterns, individual companies, and specific shapes.

Twenty years ago, not very many people would have considered Homer Laughlin's obscure line Tango collectible at all. But because of continuous exposure by Sharon and Bob Huxford in successive editions of their Fiesta books, Tango has increased significantly in value. Books on collecting are a major factor as to what becomes collectible and what doesn't.

The Manufacturers

No one knows for certain how many American potteries made dinnerware. Dozens of companies were in business for brief periods; others may have produced only one or two forgettable lines of dinnerware during two centuries of manufacturing ceramics. At the turn of the twentieth century, East Liverpool, Ohio, alone boasted approximately one hundred potteries!

But a few companies were successful and influential in the production and marketing of American dinnerware, and, for the most part, it is these potteries whose wares are collectible. Most of these have one—or several—books devoted to documenting the factory history and output along with detailed information on important lines and their designers.

Here, we'll provide brief profiles of seven top potteries. It is admittedly a subjective selection (if you collect Universal's Cattail or Royal China's Old Curiosity Shop, you probably won't agree with our choices); our criteria were quality of product, collectibility, and innovative characteristics of designs and/or patterns.

Homer Laughlin China Company

Since 1871, the Homer Laughlin China Company has been a major producer of dinnerware, operating in two locations: East Liverpool, Ohio, and across the river in Newell, West Virginia (only the latter plant remains). Today, the company constitutes the largest dinnerware manufacturer in America, known especially for its double-thick, vitrified restaurant and institutional ware.

Homer Laughlin started the company in partnership with Nathaniel Simms; later, his brother Shakespeare Laughlin was also a partner. Yet Homer Laughlin made the company a success largely on his own when both partners went on to other interests. Two lines are recognized as company signatures: Harlequin, which was sold by Woolworth stores (some items were reissued to celebrate Woolworth's 100th anniversary, in 1979); and Fiesta, still in production in a variety of colors. Fiesta is the line most widely recognized by the public today, and perhaps best defines American vintage dinnerware.

This Homer Laughlin Marigold deep plate (rimmed soup) is decorated with floral decals and a gold filigree band inside the rim. The gently scalloped edge is accented by an embossed petal design at regular intervals. "Marigold" actually refers to the light-yellow glaze. *Photo courtesy of Home Grown Antiques.*

Hall China Company

Operating in East Liverpool, Ohio, from 1903 to the present, Hall China Company has produced many dinnerware lines and extensive kitchenware assortments. Hall is known for its dozens of teapot shapes. Its major collectible dinnerware lines include Autumn Leaf, Orange Poppy, Red Poppy, and Crocus.

J. A. Bauer Pottery Company

With its roots were in Paducah, Kentucky, the J. A. Bauer Pottery Company moved to California and established a new venture there in 1909. Until the 1920s, Bauer focused on gardenware, flower-pots, and stoneware.

In 1930 the company introduced the first of its many dinner-ware lines, Plainware (commonly "Plain"), soon followed by its most famous line, Ringware (or "Ring"). Produced for nearly thirty years in bright, primary colors, Ringware was sometimes made in limited quantities, requiring later collectors to search devotedly for certain rare pieces. The line's success prompted the creation of Fiesta by the Homer Laughlin China Company in 1936. La Linda and Monterey Moderne were other popular Bauer patterns. The business closed in 1962.

Red Wing Potteries

Red Wing Potteries, of Red Wing, Minnesota, best known for its art pottery, also produced beautiful hand-painted earthenware in a variety of shapes, including crocks and jugs, from its inception in 1877. By the late 1940s the company manufactured primarily dinnerware.

Renowned designer Eva Zeisel created the offbeat and humor-ous Town and Country line for the company. Red Wing is also known for Fondoso, Futura, Chevron, and Bob White—its top seller, produced until the company closed in 1967.

Gladding McBean and Company/Franciscan

Gladding McBean and Company, founded in 1875 by Charles Gladding in Lincoln, California, first produced clay drainage pipes, then diversified into terra-cotta, hollow tiles, and bricks. In 1934, the Franciscan line of tableware went into production. Under the direction of Frederic Grant and his wife, Mary Grant, an influential designer, Franciscan became one of most successful names in American dinnerware. In 1942 the company introduced Franciscan Fine China.

El Patio was a solid-color, durable, high-quality design guaranteed to be craze resistant. Starburst, an astral, space-age design, was introduced in the 1950s and is now one of the most intensely sought lines in America. Other very collectible patterns in the Franciscan line include Coronado, Metropolitan, Apple, Desert Rose, and Ivy.

In 1984, Wedgwood Group, a new owner, closed the Franciscan plant and moved operations to Britain. As of 1999, only seven Franciscan designs were in production.

Metlox Potteries

Like other American potteries in the early '30s, Metlox Potteries of Manhattan Beach, California, produced a set of colorful informal dinnerware, California (1932). The company's origin, however, was in the manufacture of ceramic bases used in neon advertising signs.

Central Park by Metlox Poppytrail, pattern introduced in 1953.

The success of California ware encouraged an expansion into full dinnerware production under the name Poppytrail. By the mid-1950s, largely thanks to Evan K. Shaw, who purchased the

Metlox Poppytrail advertising sign. *Photo courtesy of Retrospective Modern Design.*

plant in 1946, Poppytrail was producing popular and enduring designs: California Provincial (a rooster motif), Confetti, Navajo, Aztec, and Mobile.

Metlox Potteries purchased select molds and shapes—as well as the trade name Vernonware—when the rival pottery Vernon Kilns closed suddenly in 1958. Metlox itself went out of business in 1989, after facing two decades of pressure from foreign competition and an American public that increasingly preferred inexpensive dinnerware that required little care.

California Aztec creamer (front) and gravy boat from the Freeform line by Metlox Poppytrail. *Photo courtesy of Retrospective Modern Design.*

> ### *The Fathers of American Dinnerware?*
> The mass production of American dinnerware beginning in the 1800s was
> simply a logical extension of business for many potteries. Most manufacturers
> began by closely imitating English wares. But if anyone were to be credited with
> the "invention" of American dinnerware, certainly Homer and Shakespeare
> Laughlin (whose mother obviously had a flair for the dramatic) warrant serious
> consideration for the distinction. One reason their company is so noteworthy is
> the sheer quantity of dinnerware produced in its many plants.

Contempora creamer in mist gray, designed by Ben Seibel for Raymor, manufactured by Steubenville in the late 1950s. Meant to serve as a follow-up to American Modern, Contempora met with less success and had a short period of production. *Photo courtesy of Retrospective Modern Design.*

Steubenville Pottery Company

Steubenville Pottery Company is most famous for producing
Russel Wright's American Modern dinnerware from 1939 until the
pottery closed in 1959, but its earliest products, dating from 1879,
included toilet articles.

The Woodfield line, with a distinctive leaf pattern, used the
glazes of American Modern. A Ben Seibel design, Contempora,
was produced as a successor to American Modern. This line never
achieved the popularity of Wright's dinnerware, but its modern,
subtle shapes and pattern of wavy inscribed horizontal lines have
endeared it to collectors.

The Processes

Most American dinnerware has been made in one of two forms: earthenware or china. These involve two different ways of preparing and firing clay, but there are other names for both, sometimes causing confusion. *China* is another name for *porcelain,* a clay with high silica content fired at high temperatures, resulting in a glasslike (vitrified), nonporous body. Porcelain is translucent, thin, and lightweight—yet strong and resistant to crazing and chipping.

Earthenware, or simply *pottery,* is a nonvitrified, somewhat nonporous ware. An earthenware body is fired at lower temperatures, and is often coarser and more durable than china. Earthenware can also be fired at higher temperatures, resulting in a harder body that is called semivitreous. Earthenware is opaque, often looks more informal than china, and because of its thick body, lends itself to a variety of shapes and styles, as well as raised-relief designs.

Exact manufacturing processes, including the chemical compositions used in glazes, were often considered secrets of the trade (Hall even had a line of single-fired ware called Secret Process). Russel Wright was extremely particular about the glaze tints and color effects on his dinnerware. He worked for years with pottery employees to perfect his glazes and achieve various outcomes, including a lovely raindrop or oil-spot effect within his Casual line.

Casual teapot, redesigned by Russel Wright for Iroquois. *Photo courtesy of Retrospective Modern Design.*

Shapes were created by casting (also called molding), jiggering, and pressing. In casting, liquid clay, called slip, is poured into a mold to harden into a semisoft state. Excess liquid is poured out and the hardened clay is removed from the mold, retaining its shape. It is then sent on its way to be fired, glazed, decorated, and fired again. Hollowware, or container shapes such as sugar bowls, teapots, and casseroles, are almost always made by casting.

In the jiggering process, firmer clay is placed into a half-mold, then forced to take on the mold's form by a rotating tool. Most round shapes, such as plates, cups, and lids, are made by jiggering.

Oval pieces, including bakers, serving bowls, and platters, are made by pressing. Clay in an almost hard state is put on a half-mold, then forced into the shape of the mold by a ram press.

These three means of making dinnerware were originally all performed by hand, but were eventually replaced by automation.

After being shaped (including any relief designs or sculpted edges), earthenware pieces were usually fired to create clean bisque ready for application of decoration. The most common decoration on mass-produced dinnerware was achieved with a decal—a small sheet of film containing a motif. The decal is applied to the bisque piece and then fired; during firing, the film burns away, leaving the

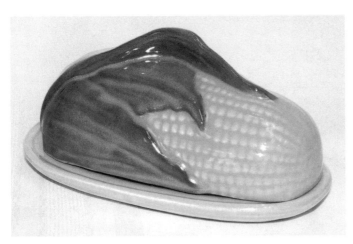

This Shawnee Corn-King butter dish comes from a popular line of molded dinnerware made from the mid-1940s to 1961, when the company closed. Shawnee was founded in 1937 in Zanesville, Ohio, and lured Addis E. Hull Jr. away from Hull Pottery to manage the new company. Corn-King, along with its related patterns—White Corn and Corn-Queen—is highly sought after, representing the perfect marriage of American art pottery and utilitarian ware. *Photo courtesy of Home Grown Antiques.*

decoration. Depending on the glaze applied over them, some decals are quite fragile and fade with time, while others hold up surprisingly well.

Other forms of decoration included hand painting (executed by human beings with paintbrushes—sometimes on tens of thousands of pieces for a popular line), silk-screening, and trims. Gold and silver (platinum) trims are very common and very easily damaged, as they are ordinarily applied over the glaze. Solid-color trims are usually applied under the glaze, then fired, and won't wear or rub off so readily.

Some of Franciscan's china was fired as many as five times, reaching temperatures of 2500°F for a period as long as eighteen hours. Metlox's Poppytrail line of earthenware, on the other hand, underwent an initial firing of 2100°F for forty hours, then was refired at 1875°F.

The maker's backstamp on the underside of a piece often reveals a wealth of information, as it does here— manufacturer, pattern, and designer. Only the date is missing.

Manufacturers' Marks

Marks are one of the joys of pottery. Most dishes of value made in the twentieth century were marked with the pattern name and the name of the manufacturer. Typically, these marks are backstamped on the bottom of the dish, but fairly frequently you'll see incised marks (Fiesta, Bauer, Hull Mirror Brown), and you may even see an embossed mark (Frankoma) or paper label on rare occasions. The six hundred pages of *Lehner's Encyclopedia of U.S. Marks on Pottery, Porcelain and Clay* are filled with examples of marks both famous and obscure. A long-lived company like Shenango is represented by more than 250 marks, some of which appear on many lines, others on only one.

Marks found on dinnerware can include everything from a company logo to the designer's name, a date code, a patent number, and the city of manufacture. Although they are usually helpful, marks can sometimes lead to problems in identification. For example, new collectors of Metlox may think the name of their pattern is Poppytrail because they see the mark "Poppytrail by Metlox." That's actually the name of the dinnerware division.

Adding to the confusion, the Poppytrail division was named after a pattern called Poppy Trail, which was Metlox's first notable success in 1934.

Patents and Copyrights

Both manufacturers and distributors of American dinnerware registered thousands of patents and copyrights to protect proprietary processes, equipment, names, marks, and designs. Following are some notable instances.

Processes. Gladding McBean and Company held a number of patents on a superior composite for earthenware and china bodies. By the time Franciscan Fine China was introduced in 1942, its chemists had developed and patented a clay mixture called Malinite, protected by both U.S. and foreign patents to this day.

Equipment. Willis Prouty, the early owner of Metlox, patented several machines that lowered production costs and improved the speed and efficiency of factory operations.

Names, marks, and designs. Filing for ownership of names, marks, and designs was standard practice at most potteries. Many company records have been lost, as fire was a common hazard. On occasion, a company might be required to alter its chosen mark. For example, in 1932, the Federal Trade Commission required the pottery company Limoges, located in Sebring, Ohio, to add the words "United States of America" to its backstamps, in order to avoid confusion between the American company's wares and the higher-quality china made by numerous companies in Limoges, France.

The Designers

A score of outstanding designers have influenced how we serve food, the time we spend in the kitchen, and, yes, even our moods at the dining table. Although some celebrated artists and illustrators designed now highly collectible dinnerware lines (such as the Famous Artists series by Vernon Kilns), here we highlight a handful of designers whose primary work was in tableware—people who were devoted to ceramics and dinnerware as art and occupation.

Russel Wright

Russel Wright designed the bestselling dinnerware in history, American Modern by Steubenville Pottery of Ohio, produced from 1939 to 1959. Wright's sleek, simple designs with subtle, natural-looking glazes revolutionized dinnerware production. The line boldly carried his name, thus spurring other designers to use similar marketing approaches. American Modern's breakthrough design and beautiful, sometimes mottled, glazes appealed to consumers so much that they often stood in long lines at department stores to be among the first to purchase new releases.

Wright's Casual by Iroquois began production in 1946. A criticism of the line's wildly successful predecessor, American Modern, was that it chipped and broke easily. Casual was designed to wear well, and it does. In fact, during in-store promotions for Casual, Wright was known to drop items on the floor to illustrate their durability. The line was redesigned five times, lastly in 1959. An experimenter and perfectionist at heart, Wright tried a variety of firing techniques, colors, and glazes on this line.

These two lines were Wright's greatest commercial successes, but he scored a critical success with White Clover for Harker, which earned him an award from the Museum of Modern Art (see page 8).

American Modern demitasse cups and saucers and reed-handled divided relish dish, designed by Russel Wright. *Photo courtesy of Retrospective Modern Design.*

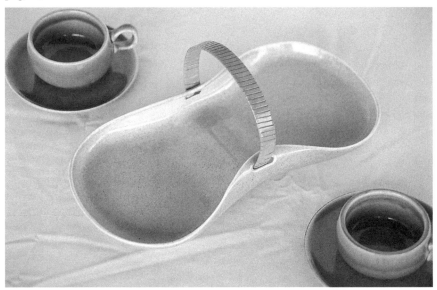

Ben Seibel

Ben Seibel's star was on the rise in the late 1950s. He was an astute marketer, and his designs superseded the simple, undecorated dinnerware Russel Wright adored. In 1952, when the famous Roseville Pottery Company was experiencing financial difficulties, Seibel was asked to design a dinnerware line that would help revive it. The result was Raymor Modern Stoneware, an undecorated line that is highly collectible now but, alas, did not save the company from failing.

Working from the 1940s into the 1980s, Seibel personally developed the shapes of his dinnerware, but the decals were the work of a number of designers in his office. Seibel's dinnerware designs were manufactured by Iroquois (Impromptu, Informal, Inheritance, and Intaglio), Steubenville (Contempora), Mikasa (a U.S. company that produces dinnerware in Japan), Pfaltzgraff (Country-Time), Roseville, and others. A few of his designs remain in production today.

Blue Diamonds bowl with teacup and saucer, from the Informal line designed by Ben Seibel for Iroquois, pattern introduced in 1958. *Photo courtesy of Retrospective Modern Design.*

Town and Country pitcher, designed by Eva Zeisel for Red Wing, pattern introduced in 1946. *Photo courtesy of Retrospective Modern Design.*

Eva Zeisel

Hungarian by birth, Eva Zeisel studied at the Royal Academy of Fine Arts in Budapest in hopes of being a painter. She decided to learn a craft in order to support her love of painting, and became a ceramist. In 1925, at age eighteen, Zeisel began her own pottery and worked in Hungary, Germany, and the Soviet Union before moving to New York in 1938.

Zeisel created notable and highly sought-after designs for Hall China, Red Wing, Castleton China, Riverside Ceramic Company, and Sears, Roebuck and Company.

In 1996 and 1997, select items from Zeisel's Town and Country line were reissued, with her permission, by World of Ceramics of Morganton, North Carolina. Most authorized revival pieces are stamped EZ96 or EZ97, to distinguish them from the originals. A different manufacturer recently reissued other Town and Country pieces for sale through the Metropolitan Museum of Art.

Mary Grant

While independent designers made a living based on name recognition, in-house designers quietly worked in pottery studios perfecting designs, altering molds, and anticipating public acceptance of patterns. One superb in-house designer was Mary Grant, who labored tirelessly for Gladding McBean and Company/Franciscan. Her husband, Frederic, was hired to lead the company's initiative in the dinnerware market in 1934. Mary, a savvy designer, stylist, and marketer, worked as chief stylist for the company until 1952.

Mary Grant's personal designs—as well as the Franciscan designs produced under her supervision—include some of today's most popular and collectible dinnerware: hand-painted Desert Rose and Ivy earthenware, and two fine-china lines she developed, Encanto and Merced. She had a strong sense of what would sell. Carmel, one pattern from her Encanto shape (chosen by the Museum of Modern Art for its 1951 design exhibition), was held back in 1948 as too modern. Upon later release, Carmel became Franciscan's biggest seller.

Desert Rose gravy boat with attached underplate, designed by Mary Grant for Franciscan. *Photo courtesy of Star Center Mall.*

Homestead Provincial pepper mill, salt mill, and eggcup designed by Bob Allen and Mel Shaw for Metlox Poppytrail. *Photo courtesy of Retrospective Modern Design.*

Bob Allen and Mel Shaw

In 1946, Metlox Potteries' new owner, Evan K. Shaw, made a monumental decision when he hired Bob Allen and Mel Shaw as art directors. Allen and Shaw came from film-studio backgrounds at MGM and Walt Disney Studios before establishing their own design firm.

The team's first Metlox design was the hand-decorated, streamlined California Ivy on coupe shapes (1946). The design's success introduced Metlox's trademark hand-decorated style and stabilized the company financially.

Allen and Shaw also designed the Provincial shape for Metlox: the highly popular Colonial scenes of Homestead Provincial (a farm scene), California Provincial (a spry rooster), and other homey Americana motifs. As the popularity of Provincial increased, so did the number of dinnerware and accessory items within each line.

The Vernon Team

Vernon Kilns employed arguably the most talented bevy of in-house designers. Gale Turnbull, Henry Bird, Jane Bennison, and sisters Mary and Vieve Hamilton all produced outstanding work for the company in the 1930s. Elliott House was yet another important Vernon designer during the 1950s.

Gale Turnbull produced several notable shapes, including Ultra—appearing in Vernon's Famous Artists series, featuring illustrations by Rockwell Kent, Don Blanding, and Walt Disney

Studios. He also designed some of the plaid lines of Vernon dinnerware and the popular Native American series, which featured images of the Southwest: mission scenes and life in Old California. He became Vernon's art director in 1936, after serving as a respected painter and engraver at Leigh Potteries and Sebring Pottery in Ohio.

Elliott House became art director in 1952 and created the Anytime shape. Decorations on this shape included Tickled Pink, a light, airy '50s pattern of small squares and crosses in pink and charcoal, and Heavenly Days, a blue-and-charcoal version. He stayed with the company until it closed in 1958.

Tickled Pink on the Anytime shape designed by Elliott House for Vernon Kilns. Photo courtesy of Retrospective Modern Design.

The Best Resources for a Quick Education

See "Resources to Further Your Collecting" on pages 111–119 for addresses and contact information on clubs, periodicals, e-groups, and so on. *Maloney's Antiques and Collectibles Resource Directory* is an excellent place to find exhaustive listings in these and other categories.

Collectors' Clubs and Associations

Whether you're trying to collect each teapot shape made by Hall or amassing examples from every line created by a favorite designer, you'll find a collectors' club devoted to your interest. From Abingdon to Watt, there is now at least one club dedicated to almost every dinnerware manufacturer. There are collecting societies for individual designers (Eva Zeisel), shapes (salt-and-pepper sets), and single patterns (Autumn Leaf). Joining one or more of these groups will further your education by leaps and bounds.

Newsletters, lectures, workshops, marketplace updates, conventions, and auctions of your specialty item are only a few of the reasons to be part of a collecting society. The group as a whole represents a repository of all the information researched over the years by fellow aficionados. Many associations catalog the factory output, preserve records and documents when a pottery goes out of business, and maintain museums and archives for members' use.

Magnolia bread plate by Stangl Pottery

Trade Papers and Magazines

The Daze is an excellent source of information on tableware of all types, including American dinnerware. Your subscription will keep you up-to-date on current news in the field. You'll find out about auctions, exhibits, and sales—and the classifieds will keep you apprised of market prices. *The Antique Trader Weekly* is a publication that will help new collectors become familiar with antiquing in general; it also offers occasional articles on dinnerware, as well as sale listings.

It bears repeating that the newsletter published by your collectors' club will be a primary and continuing part of your education. Many of these club publications include abstracts of lectures given at regional and national meetings, so even if you can't flit around the country to attend every event, you'll have access to the experts' experts.

To build your knowledge of pottery in general—not dinnerware specifically—consider subscribing to *Ceramics Monthly* and *Pottery Lovers Newsletter.* Another publication you'll want to look at if you're collecting one of the modern designers is *Echoes,* a magazine devoted to modern style, including dinnerware.

Books

You'll want to read everything you can find on dinnerware in general and your collecting specialty in particular. The experts are unanimous that the best place to start is Harvey Duke's *Official Price Guide to Pottery and Porcelain*. Despite the title, this book is much more than a price guide, providing concise histories of the major potteries in twentieth-century America, plus invaluable lists of the pieces that were available in different patterns. Carry it with you to antiques malls and flea markets, as the photos and marks will help you identify authentic pieces.

Another essential for new collectors is *The Collector's Encyclopedia of American Dinnerware* by Jo Cunningham. Historical information, color photos of different patterns, and many catalog and advertising reprints make this a must for your library.

The best reference for marks is *Lehner's Encyclopedia of U.S. Marks on Pottery, Porcelain and Clay*, by Lois Lehner. You'll find examples of every mark Lehner was able to authenticate, as well as information on dating pottery.

Beyond these basics, you'll want to add the best books on specialized topics to your library. For example:

- *Collector's Encyclopedia of Russel Wright*, by Ann Kerr. A must-have for the Wright collector. Well researched and documented.
- *Red Wing Dinnerware: Price and Identification Guide*, by Ray Reiss. This forty-page book features all Red Wing dinnerware lines, with at least one pictured example from each.
- *Franciscan: An American Dinnerware Tradition*, by Bob Page and Dale Frederiksen. Well-researched, nicely documented, thorough background information on one of America's most successful dinnerware manufacturers.

Ask other collectors for recommendations—they're a reliable indicator of which books are most authoritative. And always check facts in multiple sources—remember, just because it's in print doesn't make it true.

Web Sites and E-mail Groups

If you have access to the Internet, there are a variety of discussion groups and informational Web sites that will be invaluable.

Cocinero mixing bowl by Gladding McBean/Franciscan, produced from 1934 to 1938. *Photo courtesy of Retrospective Modern Design.*

Many collectors' associations maintain Web sites, some quite specialized: for instance, www.mindspring.com/~dway/town.html is devoted solely to Eva Zeisel's Town and Country, providing gorgeous photos and background information on this line.

Other sites are geared to provide educational background: for example, www.inter-services.com/HallChina includes a virtual tour of the Hall China factory, still in operation today. There are also lots of historic data on the company and its individual designs.

Some trade publications provide general collecting information at their sites, including: *The Antique Trader Weekly* (at www.csmonline.com/antiquetrader) and *The Daze* (at www. dgdaze.com).

E-groups are a great place to exchange information, verify facts, or locate an item you're searching for. Again, collectors' clubs often maintain these addresses. For instance, "the Official Franciscan and Gladding McBean Collectors Web Site" (at www.gmcb.com/franciscan) includes a discussion group, publications, member services, and more.

Retrospection (at www.egroups.com/subscribe/retrospection) is an e-mail list that welcomes anyone interested in mid-century modern American dinnerware. And the site provides information on an almost limitless number of e-groups and bulletin boards, devoted to every subspecialty. Many come and go, so search for current e-groups using the same keywords you use to find auctions of your favorite wares.

Pepper Tree by Metlox Poppytrail, pattern introduced in 1957.
Photo courtesy of Retrospective Modern Design.

BEFORE YOU BEGIN BUYING DINNERWARE

The Golden Rules of Collecting

Avid collectors, dealers, and longtime authorities on American dinnerware offer their best advice in this section. Many of them prefaced their comments with "If only I'd known this when I started out! I could've saved so much money (time, aggravation, disappointment)." Heed these rules for happy collecting.

1. Learn Everything You Can

Spend money on books and subscriptions before you start buying in earnest for your collection. The more you know before you begin, the better off you'll be. And always remember to check multiple sources: just because it's in print doesn't make it fact.

2. Be Patient

After you've been collecting for a while, you'll come to realize that there are more rare and desirable pieces out there than most of us could ever hope to own. Don't become desperate to add a particular piece to your collection; you'll likely see that piece over and over in the course of your collecting.

3. Buy Quality, Not Quantity

It isn't easy to resell mediocre or damaged items, so inspect merchandise carefully to avoid disappointments. Try to buy the very best you can afford. Adding a single rare or distinctive piece to your collection beats buying a dozen common ones every time.

4. Collect What You Like

Don't let anyone else's taste determine what you collect. Surround yourself with the pieces that give you pleasure.

5. Be Active

Networking with shop owners and fellow collectors is one of your best collecting strategies. It's important to continue to grow in your knowledge of the collectible and to gather firsthand experiences at a variety of outlets.

6. Be Fair

Take pride in conducting yourself in a respectful and generous manner. Usually, if you are making a purchase, a dealer will take the time to share his or her knowledge. But don't expect a busy dealer to give you an education for free.

If you ask other collectors to watch out for items on your want list, reciprocate. If they share their information and research with you, then do the same with them. Building relationships is often the key to building a great collection, and collectors reap what they sow. Your fairness and generosity to others will come back to you many times over.

7. Nurture Your Personal Vision

Collecting by rote is a lifeless pursuit. Don't let reference books, other collectors, or dealers dictate how or what you should or shouldn't collect. Look beyond the icons in the field, and let your creativity and personality guide your choices.

Out in the Marketplace

Garage, Yard, and Tag Sales

Dinnerware, glass, and clothing are the most common items found at yard sales. Don't get too excited when you read an ad touting dishes: chances are, they'll be modern-day Corelle or

---

If There's One, There's Another

Even the savviest collectors can get carried away during a heated auction. One dealer who always cautions beginners to be patient found himself forgetting his own best advice. He bid on a Homer Laughlin Brittany teapot in an online auction. They're not easy to find, so he plunged into a bidding war and ended up paying $120, which he knew was much too high a price.

Adding insult to injury, he saw a Brittany teapot with the same decoration in identical condition two weeks later in an antiques mall. The price? Ten dollars.

---

miscellaneous chipped and cracked older dishes (expect to see a lot of Homer Laughlin in that condition; it was once the preferred choice for everyday dishes). And if you see an ad that mentions Fiesta or Metlox dishes, it will attract every dealer from twenty miles around. You'll have to be first and have the fastest hands.

- Learn to recognize patterns and makers' marks so you can identify what is worth buying and what isn't.
- Sellers at garage sales often have no idea what they have, and mark "old dishes" at giveaway prices, so bargains abound. At the other extreme, sellers who recognize a famous name on their dinnerware may price a set sky-high, whether it has much value or not.
- Arrive early. Plot your route to cover as many sales as possible, and go first to the best neighborhoods in town.

Estate Sales and Auctions

Collectors searching for American dinnerware will find that estate sales and auctions are outstanding venues. You'll be in competition with a lot of dealers, but you have the advantage. A dealer must mark up merchandise at least 50 percent to make a living, but you can bid more than that and still pay less than retail.

If the estate sale has published a phone number, call ahead to see what's being sold and to ascertain that a dealer hasn't already bought the whole estate. This happens all the time, and sellers forget to cancel the ad. Always attend the preview to scrutinize any dishes you might bid on. Decide then how much you'll bid and stick to it, no matter what.

Flea Markets

The flea market is a favorite venue of many dinnerware collectors. The larger, the better. The merchandise is always changing, so be sure to tell dealers what you're looking for. If you're a regular buyer, they'll often hold merchandise for you.

At a flea market it's doubly important to inspect items carefully for damage, wear, scratches, chips, or repairs. Don't buy anything in questionable condition unless you know it is a rare or hard-to-find piece—and even then, ask yourself whether it's worth looking further for one in better condition.

Thrift and Consignment Shops

Thrift shops—where items are donated to benefit charities—may yield some fine treasures if you're dedicated enough to keep checking back. Don't ask for a discount at charity shops, although a volunteer worker may offer one if you're buying a lot.

Merchandise is sold on a commission basis in consignment shops. Salespeople aren't necessarily knowledgeable about dinnerware, so good buys are common. These shops depend upon rapid turnover, so there may be room to negotiate the price, especially if the item is near the end of its consignment period.

Introduced in 1954, the Franciscan Flair line eventually featured four patterns— Autumn (shown, introduced in 1955), Echo, Fern Dell, and Woodlore. *Photo courtesy of Retrospective Modern Design.*

Junk Shops

Junk shops will sell anything from jewelry and electronics to furniture and dinnerware. This seller will be the least likely to know what he has, thus bargains may abound. But be careful: damaged merchandise can be sold without any notation, and you're not going to be able to return that "perfect" Hall Hook Cover teapot when you discover that the hook has been broken off and glued back on.

Dealers' Web Sites

Searching for dinnerware on Web sites is fast becoming the most convenient and efficient way to build up your collection rapidly. You can enter a search for "Wallace Westward Ho dinnerware" and come up with several sites that offer the rare Wallace "cowboy" patterns. Items on dealers' Web sites are usually in outstanding condition and backed by satisfaction-guaranteed policies.

Many Web sites have a page, or a section on the home page, that explains policies regarding pricing, how to order, shipping, and, of course, returns. Be sure to read the "fine print" and ask for specifics about condition, makers' marks, and so on, before you agree to purchase.

Online Auctions

There is an abundant supply of American dinnerware up for auction on general-interest Web auction sites. As a matter of fact, it is impossible to keep up with all the auctions going on, especially when there can be more than 125,000 listings in eBay's Pottery and Glass category alone on any given day. These auctions can be extremely competitive, and sellers don't always have a clue about what they're selling. Read "Participating in Online Auctions" later in this chapter, then proceed with caution.

E-groups

Stimulating and thought-provoking discussions about designers, manufacturers, items within a line, upcoming shows, and museum exhibitions are held by e-group members, who often archive responses for permanent access.

E-groups usually include collectors and dealers looking to sell or trade. Prices will be fair market value. These people know their dinnerware, so items will be correctly identified and described. Note that it is not good e-group etiquette to ask for a discount on newly posted items; if they remain unsold, then you can make a lower offer.

Mexicana is the most common of Homer Laughlin's Mexican-theme patterns, introduced in 1937. Here, it is applied to the Century shape, designed in 1931 by Frederick Hurten Rhead, who later created Fiesta. Mexicana is one of several decal designs available on the Century shape against a "vellum" background; colored glazes were also applied to the shape for the Riviera line. The dish shown is what the company called a deep plate, or rimmed soup bowl. *Photo courtesy of Home Grown Antiques.*

Painted Desert butter dish by Metlox Poppytrail, pattern introduced in 1960. Photo courtesy of Retrospective Modern Design.

Antiques-and-Collectibles Malls

Antiques-and-collectibles malls rent space to dealers, who may or may not also pay a commission on sales. The number of dealers can be anywhere from ten to a hundred, so don't assume that what you see in the first booth or two is representative.

Pricing is almost always negotiable. Some malls leave discounts up to individual dealers; some have a mall policy, perhaps discounting 10 percent on items over $20 and 15 percent on purchases over $50. Always ask—no one is likely to volunteer a discount!

Individual Antiques Shops

Individual antiques shops often have a particular flavor that reflects the taste and personality of the owner. If you find one devoted to dinnerware and glassware, you'll have discovered a dealer who can help to educate you, as well as find those special items you need to round out a collection.

Obviously, it's worth the effort also to visit general antiques shops: you'll find that some will stock dinnerware, others won't.

Antiques-and-Collectibles Shows

Specialized shows offer unique opportunities to learn about American dinnerware, although there are only a handful of them (see "Resources to Further Your Collecting" on pages 111–113). One wonderful show is the American Pottery, Earthenware and China Show and Sale held in Springfield, Illinois, each year. A number of regional pottery shows will feature dinnerware, so watch for ads and read your club newsletters.

General antiques shows are much more numerous than specialized shows, and are also a boon to collectors. Dealers travel from all over the country, usually with their best merchandise, so this is the place to find the quality and rarity that may be lacking in your local stores. Both buyers and sellers at these shows are likely to know their dinnerware and its value.

Dealing with Dealers

Dealers are such an important source of valuable information, as well as of collectible pieces, that it pays to cultivate relationships with them. Your dealer network will pay big dividends in building a quality collection.

Can I rely on dealers to know everything about their merchandise?

No dealer can be expected to know everything about everything. In fact, it's to your advantage that they don't. You can snag real bargains on the occasions when you happen to know more about an item than the dealer who's selling it.

Dealer knowledge varies widely. Savvy collectors ask questions—lots of them. When you do that, you'll soon get a sense of whether the dealer knows what he's talking about. Specifically, ask why an item is priced as it is. The dealer should be able to give you a context for the asking price: book value, what the dealer paid for it, or a combination of factors. Most dealers generally are seeking to double their money at least. By asking a dealer to explain the price, you may open the door for negotiation.

That said, it rarely pays to call attention to a dealer's error—even when you know you're right. Always remain polite and nonargumentative. Listen to everything the dealer says, then evaluate the truth and logic of what you hear. That way you're building bridges, instead of burning them.

Are most dealers honest?

Fortunately, yes. Dealers who habitually lie to their customers don't stay in business long. Dealers aren't out to cheat people, but those who carry a variety of merchandise may not be experts on dinnerware. It's possible for a dealer to overlook damage or to be snookered himself or herself by a reproduction.

As a new collector, you'll rarely go wrong if you stick with dealers who've built solid reputations. Ask around, especially among fellow collectors. The more reputable the dealer, the more likely he will be to accommodate you if he unknowingly misrepresented an item you purchased.

Are prices negotiable?

Certainly. Never be afraid to bargain—it's part of the fun of collecting. Most dealers factor "wiggle room" into the asking price—anywhere from 10 to 20 percent. However, many extend discounts only on cash purchases, so don't expect a special deal when using your credit card. Always carry cash or a checkbook when antiquing.

COLLECTOR'S COMPASS
Want-List Wonders

An up-to-date want list in the hands of a dealer who knows you is your best route to finding the pieces you need. It doesn't obligate you to buy, but before you cast your list to the four winds, consider the prices you're willing to pay for the items you've put on it. Sometimes it's better not to attach prices—you may get a better deal than you anticipated!

You should, however, be prepared to pay typical market prices for the items on your want list. This doesn't necessarily mean top dollar, but you'll find that dealers seldom call collectors who are looking only for "wholesale-price steals."

Keep your negotiations positive. You can and should point out flaws not clearly acknowledged by an "as is" or "as found" on the price tag. Any dealer can miss a crack or chip, and condition is a big consideration in collecting dinnerware or pottery. But don't expect to negotiate a terrific price by disparaging the merchandise.

If you're interested in a piece that's too expensive, casually test the waters: "I really like this, but I can't pay what you're asking." A more direct approach is simply to ask, "Would you be open to an offer?" or "Is this your best price?"

The more time you invest in your discussion with the dealer, the better your chances of achieving your target price. If the two of you reach common ground, be prepared to buy. There are few things more aggravating to a dealer than a customer who negotiates as a game, with no real intention of buying.

> **"I'll Take It!"**
>
> On those supremely memorable occasions when you happen across a sought-after item that's ridiculously underpriced, simply say "I'll take it!"
>
> Don't discuss. Don't negotiate. Just buy it and walk away. The dealer almost certainly will eventually realize his mistake. And although it's fair to buy a bargain, don't add insult to injury by asking for an additional discount.

Is it a good idea to leave a "standing bid" with a dealer for a particular piece I want?

A standing bid—the highest price you're willing to pay—can actually work against you. A dealer might use your open-ended offer to "shop the piece around," or try to tease out interest at a higher price. Instead, make it a one-time offer: "I'll buy this piece right now for this price." Of course, that doesn't mean you wouldn't buy it later for the same price, but such a statement might prompt the dealer to act.

Should I request a receipt for every purchase?

Yes, definitely. Be sure it includes the dealer's name and address, your name, and a description of the piece you've bought (including its approximate age and condition). The exceptions: garage or yard sales and flea markets, where vendors may not give receipts; at these venues, simply record the details of your purchase in a notebook.

Don't be surprised when your receipt shows an amount added for sales tax. Dealers are required to include it and, increasingly, state agencies are monitoring compliance.

What recourse do I have if I'm not satisfied with a purchase?

Most dealers will not accept returns on dinnerware, glassware, and other breakables unless you can prove that an item sold is something other than what it was represented to be. Always ask about a dealer's return policy, especially when buying through the mail. A receipt that describes the item is your first line of defense. If you discover that the piece isn't authentic, you've got something in writing to back up your claim.

Carefully inspect every piece before you buy it, and specifically ask the dealer questions about its condition, the originality of all parts (lids, etc.), and any history of repair. One common reason for dealers not to accept returns is that it's easy for unscrupulous buyers to substitute low-quality or damaged merchandise for the original purchase. Unfortunately, these things happen, and the honest buyers are penalized for them.

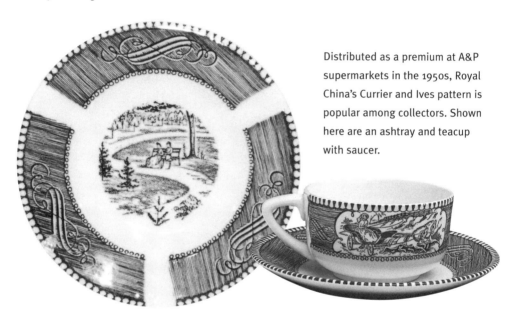

Distributed as a premium at A&P supermarkets in the 1950s, Royal China's Currier and Ives pattern is popular among collectors. Shown here are an ashtray and teacup with saucer.

Participating in Online Auctions

Where can I find online auctions?

eBay is arguably the most popular auction site on the Internet. When you call up the home page, at www.ebay.com, you'll see that the site is organized by items of interest. Whether you're a buyer or a seller, there are buttons you can click for help and additional information.

Amazon.com and Yahoo Auctions are two other rapidly growing online auction sites. By visiting a popular search engine such as www.google.com and entering "online auction" as your search term, you'll generate a long list of other sites to check out, too.

How do I register for an online auction?

On eBay, one of the first headings you'll see on the home page is for a "New User" section. This explains the details of bidding and selling, both of which require you to register (you must have an e-mail address). Access the registration page, and enter your personal information. The eBay registration page can be found at: http://pages.ebay.com/services/registration/register.html.

In order to sell items, you have to place a credit-card number on file. There's usually a small fee for placing an item on auction, and a commission when the item is sold. These charges are made directly to your credit-card account. You'll also receive a monthly statement of charges from the online auction.

How do I search for items I'm interested in?

Begin your search with a category: pottery, dinnerware, tableware, kitchenware. Next, narrow it to the type of dinnerware that you collect by selecting a manufacturer or style of dishes: Bauer, Bennington, Brayton Laguna. You can then do a keyword search within the subcategory for the specific piece you need. This will save you from wading through thousands of unrelated items. The savvy searcher also will try less obvious terms that may locate misnamed or misspelled items: "Poppytrail cookie jar" or "Franciscan Dessert Rose" (correctly Poppy Trail and Desert Rose).

Sculptured Grape one-quart vegetable dish with lid and platter, by Metlox's Poppytrail division. *Photo courtesy of Retrospective Modern Design.*

Theme Informal, a very rare design by Russel Wright, manufactured by Yamato of Japan and imported by Schmid International. *Photo courtesy of Retrospective Modern Design.*

Another good way to find items is to bookmark your favorite sellers' lists. You can see what auctions they're conducting without having to search the keywords. It's just one more way to be a step ahead of the competition.

What are the best strategies for bidding?

Some folks like to open at the start of an auction with the highest price they're willing to pay, in order to discourage others from bidding. Other bidders prefer to wait until the last possible moment before the auction closes. This guarantees that your best bid will either win or lose, and you won't be tempted to keep bidding.

But remember that other bidders can use the auction search feature to see what other items you're bidding on. If you're seeking modern-designer dinnerware, another bidder can use your bid list to track down items he otherwise might not find. By waiting until the last moment to bid, you minimize this method of discovery.

One of the early Ohio River Valley potteries was W. S. George, which operated at East Palestine from 1904 until the late 1950s. This rare teapot, with an eighteenth-century courtship scene, was probably decorated for a retail outlet or department store. *Photo courtesy of Home Grown Antiques.*

On the other hand, it can be beneficial to enter a low bid early on in an auction in order to "bookmark" it. eBay sends you an e-mail notifying you that your bid has been registered and of the closing time of the auction. It will send you another e-mail if your bid is topped by another bidder. These prompts help you monitor the auction's progress and keep track of when it closes, so you won't forget to enter that last-minute bid.

The practice of waiting until the last moment to bid, called sniping, is considered unfair by some, though it's not a violation of most online-auction rules. Some newer auction sites prevent sniping altogether by automatically extending the auction deadline if a bid comes in at the last minute.

What are reserve prices?

The minimum bid is the amount where bidding begins, but sometimes a seller also sets a reserve price, which is the lowest amount he is willing to accept. This amount isn't disclosed (unless the

Vernon Kilns Rose-a-Day teapot. *Photo courtesy of Retrospective Modern Design.*

seller chooses to reveal it in his descriptive copy), but if the item reaches its reserve price the listing will indicate that the reserve is met, and the item will be sold to the highest bidder over the reserve price.

If you want to know the seller's reserve price before bidding, send an e-mail. Some sellers will tell, some won't, but it never hurts to ask!

How does the transaction take place if my bid wins?

Once the auction closes, the site will notify both the successful bidder and the seller. After that, there is a short time within which the seller should send the successful bidder an e-mail explaining shipping and payment options. If he does not, however, you should e-mail him.

Never send your credit-card number in an e-mail! Request and be ready to pay for insurance on your purchase. And remember that your backing out of a winning bid can result in negative feedback on the auction site, and eventually, for repeated offenses, to your exclusion from bidding.

Once you've made payment and received the item, notify the seller that it arrived in good condition. When the transaction is complete, each party should post feedback on the other's profile. If you made prompt payment and abided by the auction rules, the seller should give you positive feedback. If the item was as described, the seller shipped the item promptly, packaged it suffi-ciently, and worked to resolve any disputes, then it's customary to give the seller positive feedback.

Tamac of Oklahoma eggcup and juice jug. Tamac (1948–72) was started by two Oklahoma couples. Using a durable white Georgia clay for its bodies, Tamac produced dinnerware and decorative pottery in glazes with evocative names like butterscotch, frosty pink, frosty fudge, raspberry, and honey. *Photo courtesy of Retrospective Modern Design.*

What if my purchase arrives and it isn't what was described?

If the item was misrepresented, the seller should let you return it and refund your money, but don't delay: contact the seller immediately. If your purchase was accurately described and you're simply unhappy with it, or changed your mind, you're probably stuck with it. If, by some chance, a seller does allow you to return the unwanted merchandise, be prepared to pay return shipping. If the item was damaged in shipment, notify the seller immediately to initiate a claim with the shipping entity—the post office or parcel service, as the case may be.

What are the pros and cons of buying this way?

Online auctions provide greater access to collectibles than ever before, leveling the playing field. Still, some collectors are justifiably nervous about the unsecured nature of online transactions. It takes a lot of trust to bid solely on the basis of a digital photo and a text description, and often with no guarantee. Payment must be sent to a stranger before the item is even shipped, and if you're unhappy with it, you may have limited recourse.

What's That You're Selling?

Remember that sellers on the Internet may have only a glimmer of an idea what they're selling. One collector bid on "four soup bowls" in Russel Wright's Casual by Iroquois in "oyster." When the shipment arrived, she discovered that the "oyster" items were actually pink! Moreover, three of the "soup bowls" were really cereal bowls. She returned them, insured, the same day they arrived, and notified the seller that the items were misrepresented. The seller acknowledged that she knew little about dinnerware and made a full refund.

Coors Rosebud utility jar with lid, manufactured from 1934 to 1942. The pottery that became Coors Porcelain Company was founded in 1908 by a former Roseville employee. The company is best known among collectors for its Rosebud line. *Photo courtesy of Retrospective Modern Design.*

It's smart to check the feedback on the seller before bidding, to see what the last several buyers had to say. Also, many sellers are experienced dealers and may have a link to a Web site. By following the link, you can see what kind of Internet "storefront" they have, how long they've been selling online, and judge their overall professionalism.

Sooner or later, you'll encounter sellers who don't know what they're talking about, may not know how to inspect dinnerware to assess condition, and don't know how to pack delicate dishes. But even with all the things that can potentially go wrong, the majority of transactions turn out well for both buyer and seller. Just don't hesitate to ask detailed questions about condition or to request additional photos before bidding. Ask for a guarantee that you'll be able to return the piece for a refund if it's not in the condition advertised. And save copies of all e-mail. After you get the hang of it, buying in Internet auctions is fun, and that's what collecting is all about.

Photo Gallery

Metropolitan chop plate in coral and coffee server in gray by Franciscan, pattern introduced in 1940. *Photo courtesy of Retrospective Modern Design.*

Fiesta, Designed by Frederick Hurten Rhead for Homer Laughlin China Company
This hugely successful pattern was introduced in 1936. Affordable, sturdy, and stylish, the mix-and-match dinnerware allowed consumers to create vibrant, versatile table settings.

Red, cobalt, light green, and yellow led the way upon the line's release, with ivory soon following. In 1937 Homer Laughlin added a sixth color, turquoise. Red was retired in 1943.

Light green, cobalt, and ivory were retired in 1951, with chartreuse, forest green, rose, and gray—the '50s colors—taking their places and lasting through 1959. Medium green arrived in 1959, when red was reinstated, and by 1960 Fiesta was back to just four colors: red, yellow, turquoise, and medium green.

The Fiesta backstamp. Note the use of "Genuine" to distinguish the real thing from its imitators.

Fiesta stick-handled creamer and sugar in yellow

Fiesta Kitchen Kraft serving fork in light green and cake server in red

Fiesta Tom and Jerry mugs (also called coffee mugs). Clockwise from middle rear: yellow, turquoise, light green, red, forest green, cobalt, and ivory (at center).

Fiesta fruit bowl in turquoise

Fiesta stamp on light green fruit bowl

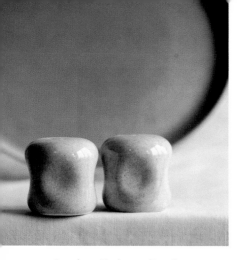

American Modern salt and pepper shakers in granite gray, with dinner plate in background

American Modern, Designed by Russel Wright for Steubenville Pottery Company

American Modern was produced from 1939 to 1959. Its breakthrough design and beautiful, often mottled glazes appealed to consumers so much that many often stood in long lines at department stores to purchase it. Colors were designed to mix and match, increasing the pattern's flexibility and appeal. *Photos courtesy of Retrospective Modern Design.*

American Modern cups and saucers in black chutney and coral

American Modern demitasse in seafoam

American Modern dinner plate and lug soup bowl in coral

PHOTO GALLERY

Casual, Designed by Russel Wright for Iroquois China Company
Created after the popular American Modern line was criticized for chipping easily, crazing, and breaking, Casual is admirably durable. The line was redesigned five times during its 1947–66 production run, with the last redesign occurring in 1959.
Photos courtesy of Retrospective Modern Design.

Earliest design Casual coffee cup and saucer in ice blue

Casual redesigned creamer in ripe apricot

Casual original stacking sugar-and-creamer set in ice blue

Casual original mugs in ice blue, charcoal, and pink. While all original mugs are favorites with collectors, the charcoal mug in the center is especially valued due to its rarity.

69

Pfaltzgraff aimed to create "authentic nineteenth-century reproductions," as illustrated by this pitcher-and-bowl set in the Yorktowne pattern. Pfaltzgraff has been around since 1811, and Yorktowne's blue floral decoration on a matte gray background harks back to the company's early salt-glazed stoneware. The pattern was produced from 1967 until the late 1990s, during which time the design changed from a Pennsylvania Dutch tulip to two blossoms sprouting from several leaves. Yorktowne has proved to be one of the most popular lines of oven-safe dinnerware of all time. *Photo courtesy of Home Grown Antiques.*

"**Frankoma**" is a combination of the pottery owner's last name, Frank, and its location, Oklahoma. Regional interest attracts many collectors to Frankoma dinnerware, but the variety of glazes and the Americana themes are also appealing.

Frankoma Wagon Wheel creamer in desert gold, made from 1941 to 1983. *Photo courtesy of Home Grown Antiques.*

Frankoma glaze and pattern sampler (clockwise from rear): desert gold Plainsman platter, woodland moss Westwind cup, white sand Mayan-Aztec shakers, flame Lazybones soup mug, brown satin Lazybones cup, and (center) prairie green Plainsman teapot. *Photo courtesy of Home Grown Antiques.*

J. A. Bauer Pottery Company

In 1933 designer Louis Ipsen added a ridged pattern to Bauer's previously smooth California Colored Pottery, and the classic Ring line was born. *Photos courtesy of Star Center Mall.*

Gloss Pastel Kitchenware cookie jar in yellow, designed by Ray Murray for Bauer. The wider spacing of the ridges, which grow broader as they move from the base to the top, distinguish Gloss Pastel Kitchenware (GPK) from Ringware. GPK was introduced in 1941.

Classic Ringware. Shown here: 9" dinner plate in royal (cobalt) blue and 12" chop plate in Chinese yellow.

Starburst gravy boat with attached underplate. The Starburst decal was designed by Mary Brown. The pattern was introduced in 1954 and manufactured into the early 1960s. *Photo courtesy of Star Center Mall.*

Eclipse candleholders with Starburst creamer and covered sugar bowl. *Photo courtesy of Retrospective Modern Design.*

The Franciscan Eclipse Shape

Designed by George James in the 1950s, the Eclipse shape was decorated with four decal designs — Duet, Pomegranate, Oasis, and Starburst.

Oasis salt and pepper shakers and creamer with platter in the background, pattern introduced in 1955. *Photo courtesy of Retrospective Modern Design.*

Duet coffee mug, platter, six-ounce tumbler, and teacup with saucer, pattern introduced in 1956. *Photos courtesy of Star Center Mall.*

Hand-Painted Franciscan

Ivy tumbler, mug, and covered casserole, pattern introduced in 1948

Desert Rose
covered sugar and
creamer, pattern
introduced in 1941

Apple 12⅝" platter and teacup with saucer, pattern introduced in 1940

All photos this page courtesy of Star Center Mall.

Salt and Pepper Shakers

Franciscan Apple.
*Photo courtesy of
Star Center Mall.*

Iroquois Casual stacking shakers in pink, charcoal, ice blue, and lemon yellow. *Photo courtesy of Retrospective Modern Design.*

Franciscan Ivy

Universal shakers
with floral decal.
*Photo courtesy of
Home Grown
Antiques.*

Homer Laughlin Fiesta
in light green

Ben Seibel

Lazy Daisy samovar, from the Informal line designed by Ben Seibel for Iroquois China Company, pattern introduced in 1958. Decal decorations like Lazy Daisy were popular in the mid '50s to early '60s, when consumers' enthusiasm for undecorated earthenware faded.

Raymor Modern Stoneware creamer (lid not shown) in terra cotta, with autumn brown and beach gray plates in the background, designed by Seibel for Roseville Pottery Company

Harvest Time milk pitcher from the Informal line

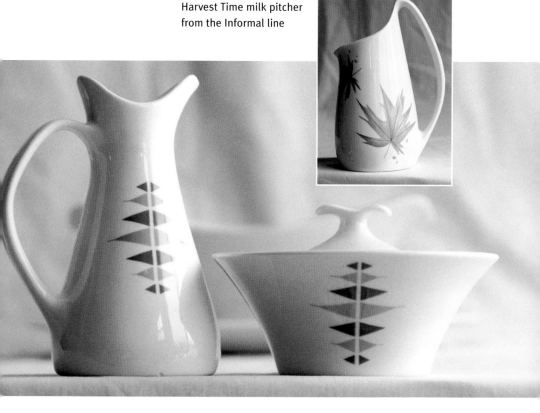

Pyramids creamer and covered sugar, from the Impromptu line designed by Seibel for Iroquois

All photos this page courtesy of Retrospective Modern Design.

Mandalay coffeepot on the Museum shape designed by Eva Zeisel for Castleton China. Originally sold through the Museum of Modern Art without decoration in 1945, the Museum shape was later adorned with decals, the Mandalay design being just one of many. In addition, Museum was used for an art series; Pablo Picasso, Marc Chagall, and Andrew Wyeth were among those commissioned to design decals. Production for this shape ended in the 1960s.

All photos this page and opposite courtesy of Retrospective Modern Design.

Town and Country creamer, cruet, and covered sugar in chartreuse, designed by Zeisel for Red Wing Potteries, pattern introduced in 1946. Town and Country pieces are unmarked, so collectors must identify them by their glazes and organic shapes.

Hallcraft sugar bowl and teacup with saucer, designed by Zeisel for Hall China Company. Hallcraft used various decal designs: Bouquet, Mulberry, Fantasy, Harlequin, and Romance (shown here).

Hallcraft Bouquet gravy boat and serving platter in the Tomorrow's Classic shape designed by Zeisel for Hall China Company

Plaids

Gay Plaid tumbler, coffee server, and covered onion soup bowl with stick handle by Blair Ceramics, a small pottery that operated in Ozark, Missouri. *Photo courtesy of Retrospective Modern Design.*

Blue Ridge Rustic Plaid 9½" dinner plate by Southern Potteries. *Photo courtesy of Star Center Mall.*

Vernon Kilns plaids of the late '30s through '50s were one of the California pottery's most popular pattern groups. Shown here: Organdie Plaid drip-cut syrup, Tam O'Shanter individual chicken pie (lid not shown) and flowerpot, and Gingham mug. *Photo courtesy of Retrospective Modern Design.*

Radiance four-piece bowl set in cheerful colors by Hall China

Butter dish in Aristocrat by Hall China

Ball jug by
Hall China

Autumn Leaf teacup and saucer.
Probably the most famous of
Hall's patterns, Autumn Leaf was
distributed as a premium by the
Jewel Tea Company. The pattern
was produced from 1933 through
the 1970s.

*All photos this page courtesy
of Star Center Mall.*

Coronado turquoise teacup and bread plate by Franciscan

NOW THAT YOU'RE READY TO START COLLECTING

Collector's Toolbox

You won't need a lot of fancy tools to examine and authenticate dinnerware in the field, but a few items will come in handy.

The most overlooked basic tool is your own hand. Measure your hands: if, for example, the length from the end of your out-stretched thumb to the tip of your index finger is 7", you can make a quick hand measurement of plate diameters, cup heights, and so on before getting out your tape measure.

Keep the following in a kit in your car (you never know when you'll stumble over a tag or estate sale).

- **Flashlight.** More often than not, places where dishes have been packed away are poorly lit—attics, basements, garages, even the shelves and cabinets of antiques shops. A flashlight will help you spot otherwise hard-to-see wear and damage.
- **Magnifying glass.** Useful for close inspection of damage, repairs, trademarks and logos, and the like.
- **Cleaning supplies.** Wet wipes, paper towels, or soft cloths and a spray bottle of glass cleaner will help you remove dust and dirt so you can examine the ware underneath—and clean your hands afterward.

- **Tape measure.** Invest in a small one that fits on a key chain; you'll need it to distinguish between Bauer Ringware's black 5" bread-and-butter plate (worth $100) and the 6" bread-and-butter plate (worth only $30 to $40). Diameters in some collectible services vary by as little as ¼".
- **Notepad and pen or pencil.** Making notes for yourself is a must when previewing auctions or when making purchases at yard or garage sales where you're not likely to get a receipt.
- **Wrapping materials.** Last, but not least, keep bubble wrap, masking tape, and small boxes in the trunk of your car. You'll thank yourself every time you come across an unexpected sale.

Determining Value

Prices realized in online auctions, as well as published book prices, will usually be reliable indicators of the value of authentic pieces in excellent to near-mint condition. But when you're out in the marketplace, how do you apply your research to the piece at hand?

Here, experts rank the factors that commonly affect value, to help you make judgments about adding individual pieces to your collection.

Condition

Impact on Value: High

Condition is extremely important in determining value. However, dinnerware was made to be used, and, for the most part, it was. Not many collectors limit themselves to mint-condition dinnerware (their collections would be tiny indeed).

Most dishes for sale in the secondary market (excluding garage and rummage sales) are in excellent to near-mint condition. If you're patient and diligent, you can build a fine collection without spending a fortune.

- **Normal usage wear.** Scratches, mainly from utensils, and small chips, commonly called fleabites, fall into the category of normal wear. There are collectors who find even one small scratch enough to make an item unattractive, but these signs of light wear, so long as they are noticeable only on close examination, do not adversely affect value. Dark, solid-color dishes (such as black and cobalt), or dishes with decals, tend to show scratches much more prominently than lighter colors like yellow and ivory.

- **Unusual usage wear.** Deep or obvious utensil scratches, or wear that has dulled or damaged the luster of the glaze, are unacceptable to most collectors and decrease value markedly. Sometimes plates or bowls have been used underneath flower-pots. Such items may have developed discolored mineral rings from standing water, and the glaze is usually compromised. Dinnerware that has repeatedly been through the dishwasher will also suffer damage to its finish. Avoid pieces with unusual wear.

- **Cracks and large chips.** Once a piece is cracked, it can almost never be used. Cracked vessels can't hold liquids reliably; any cracked piece can leach lead into certain foods. As with any type of damage, the more noticeable and numerous the flaws, the lower the value. A ½" hairline crack on a $100 salad bowl may only reduce the value to $90, while a 6" hairline crack on a 9" dinner plate will reduce the value from $12 to lucky-to-sell-for-$1. Large chips decrease the value of a piece on average by at least 50 percent.

- **Crazing.** Crazing, the fine cracks in the glaze commonly seen on older dinnerware, is a result of the clay body shrinking at a faster or slower rate than the glaze. If it is not disfiguring, crazing ordinarily doesn't decrease value, but some collectors won't tolerate it.

- **Missing paint.** Metallic or colored trims tend to wear away easily on dinnerware. Metallic trims, including the platinum or gold rims common to many patterns from the '30s and '40s, are more susceptible to wear and damage because they are generally applied over the protective glaze. For this reason, if you have a pattern with metallic trim, such as Homer Laughlin's Virginia Rose, don't put it in the dishwasher.

- **Missing parts.** The biggest mistake made by new collectors is to buy items missing their lids. Don't! Sugars, casseroles, teapots, and coffeepots without lids are in abundant—and cheap—supply, and people often think they'll eventually find a matching lid. But when the finials or knobs broke, folks discarded the lids and kept the bases, since they could still be used. If the base was broken, both it and the lid were summarily thrown out; thus, not many lids survived.

One experienced dealer says, "I can always tell a beginner when the first few items on his want list are lids. Advanced collectors know better."

The best advice is to be patient, and wait until you find a complete piece. If you do buy an incomplete piece, the price for an odd base should be low (40 percent of value for a complete piece), but for a lid should be higher (about 60 percent of value for the complete piece if it's in a common pattern; even higher if it's a rare piece). If you ever find an odd lid at a good price, grab it up. Even if you don't use it to replace a less-than-perfect lid, it's one item you should be able to resell at a gain without difficulty.

- **Repairs and restoration.** "Loving hands at home" repairs nearly always render a dish worthless to anyone but its owner. Professional restorations of unusual or rare items are acceptable. Pros can repair hairline cracks, nicks, and chips, or

---

Evaluating Condition

There is no formal rating system for American dinnerware condition, such as exist for many other collectibles. However, there is a fairly universal "industry standard":

- **Mint.** Pristine, absolutely no wear or flaws (including factory flaws). Sometimes found in original packaging, unopened.
- **Near mint.** Outstanding condition, but may have been slightly used. Insignificant wear or flaws, with the luster of the glaze fully intact.
- **Excellent.** Outstanding condition, but may show minimal wear from normal use. Light scratches are permissible, if not noticeable except under strong light. Very light crazing that is difficult to detect is allowed on more rare or unusual pieces.
- **Good.** No chips or cracks, but the dish has incurred wear that is visible to the naked eye or has noticeable compromise to the glaze. Most experts do not recommend buying items in good condition.
- **Fair.** Extensive wear, dulling or damage to the glaze. May exhibit nicks, big chips, or hairline cracks. Don't buy dishes in this condition.

freshen decorative elements. A seller must always disclose the repair, and any repair decreases resale value.

There is such a sufficiency of dinnerware in excellent condition that it's best to pass up a repaired piece. If you do buy an extraordinary example that's been repaired, don't pay more than 20 to 30 percent of its fair market value in pristine condition.

Intrinsic Characteristics

Impact on Value: High

Unusual design or detailing with eye appeal usually make a pattern a standout. One such example is the space-age Fantasy line, designed by Eva Zeisel and manufactured by Hall China Company.

Intrinsic characteristics of materials and craftsmanship augment value and desirability as well. The high quality of the earthenware used by Metlox for its dinnerware has enhanced its collectibility. And there is a large group of aficionados who value any and all hand-painted designs.

Hallcraft Fantasy cup and saucer on the Tomorrow's Classic shape designed by Eva Zeisel for Hall China Company. *Photo courtesy of Retrospective Modern Design.*

Color often becomes an important criterion in assessing value. It is especially critical among collectors of Fiesta, American Modern, and Roseville Raymor, but is also crucial to many other people who concentrate on lines of solid-color dishes. Thus, don't be surprised to find marked differences in values where color is the only variable.

Intrinsic characteristics that detract from value include traditional designs on modern shapes. These aesthetic "mismatches" simply don't appeal to sophisticated collectors. Also, low-quality clay bodies that tend to craze or chip, and dishes with decorations or glazes that damage easily are judged mostly by their design importance. They may be more or less valuable depending on their rarity and, more often, their condition.

Raymor Modern Stoneware (creamer shown without cover). In 1952, when Roseville Pottery Company was experiencing financial difficulties, Ben Seibel was commissioned to design a dinnerware line that would help revive the company. Raymor Modern Stoneware was the result. While this dinnerware didn't save Roseville, it did help Seibel make his mark in the design world. *Photo courtesy of Retrospective Modern Design.*

Original Packaging and Labeling
Impact on Value: Added

Original packaging with maker, distributor, and date is a bonus for advanced collectors. Original boxes were seldom kept after the buyer unpacked the dishes. Manufacturers sometimes used stickers on their wares, and these, too, are a bonus when intact. But the condition of the dishes themselves, as well as completeness if they are a set, will be the primary determinant of value. If all else is in order, expect to pay a premium if original packaging or stickers are part of the deal.

Amateur Decorations

It's not uncommon to find vintage pieces—especially plates—that were decorated by their owners. You should have no difficulty distinguishing them from hand-painted production ware, since amateur decorations are usually applied over the glaze. Some collectors search them out as one-of-a-kind examples of folk-art painting.

Age
Impact on Value: High, with Qualification

As previously noted, there are some lovely sets of very old dishes around that have little market value because they're not in demand. Old alone does not equal valuable. That said, age is important to most collectors as a way of identifying and authenticating dinnerware.

Potteries dated their products in different ways. An excellent reference is *Lehner's Encyclopedia of U.S. Marks on Pottery, Porcelain and Clay.*

From 1920 until the late 1950s, most pottery companies used one company backstamp for all their individual dinnerware lines. Those stamps may have been modified or changed completely at various points in the companies' histories, which will help you pinpoint the age of a particular piece using an authoritative reference like *Lehner's,* which shows and dates all the variations.

Franciscan
stamp used
from 1949 to
February 1953

The Homer Laughlin China Company was exceptional in that it used a special mark for the Fiesta line (which was changed over time), but other HLC designs had backstamps that included date codes: a piece marked B 48 N 8 establishes that the piece was made in February 1948 at Plant 8.

Knowles, Taylor Smith and Taylor, and Crooksville used simple date codes, supplying the month and year. Red Wing and Harker never used date codes, but learning the different shapes they produced over the years will help you determine an approximate date.

Familiarity with company logos and trademarks also helps you to establish age. Taylor Smith and Taylor used a griffin backstamp before 1910, so TS&T collectors can identify an early piece. Vintage ads are extremely helpful, too. They often give you three vital pieces of information: the name of the dinnerware (because retailers identified the patterns by name), how it was marketed, and its age. Retail catalogs, such as those issued by Montgomery Ward and Sears, Roebuck and Co., as well as wholesale catalogs are excellent; they were issued seasonally and are always dated. These are among the primary reference materials used by writers on collectibles.

Age can also be determined by the colors, treatments, and shapes. Once you've studied all the reference materials you can locate on your subspecialty, you'll realize that there are dozens of clues to age, manufacturer, and originality.

Rarity

Impact on Value: High

While there are hardly as many rare items as some dealers and collectors would like you to believe, certainly there are rarities in dinnerware, usually the result of limited production.

Vernon Kilns' famous series by painter Rockwell Kent, Salamina, was named after a Kent book about a legendary woman of Greenland. The dinnerware featured colorful scenes of life in the polar north. Incredibly, this line bombed, and many sets were returned to the factory, where they were destroyed. Because Salamina was discontinued so quickly, there were never many sets available. Today, these dishes are highly sought after by both dinnerware collectors and Rockwell Kent collectors, who consider the dinnerware a prized possession.

Colors can be rare if they were discontinued shortly after introduction. Medium-green Fiesta was introduced in 1959, more than twenty years after the first colors were available, and at about the same time that some shapes were being dropped. As a result, certain items are almost impossible to find: the medium-green Fiesta cream soup bowl is worth more than $3,000 because so few were made.

Some delightful lines of dishes originally intended for children are rare because they were so often broken.

COLLECTOR'S COMPASS

If an item contains the manufacturer's date code for 1950, then the most you can establish is that the blank—undecorated and unglazed greenware—was made in that year. After the code was incised or stamped on the greenware, blanks sat on shelves until needed, which might be immediately or years later. Date codes are a reliable indicator of when the actual piece was made, but not when it was decorated, shipped, or purchased.

If the backstamp says:	then the dish was made:
"dishwasher safe"	after ca. 1965
"microwave safe"	after 1980
"lead free"	after ca. 1990

Limited-edition pieces occasionally are rare and coveted. The National Autumn Leaf Collectors' Club commissioned Hall China in 1989 to produce special pieces for members only. Production was limited to the number ordered by members, and these items command premium prices. The 892 pairs of candle-holders sold exclusively to members that year for $21 now bring $225 to $250 per set.

The best sources for information about what is and isn't rare are published reference books. Books on individual lines or pottery companies usually discuss key items. Also, Web sites oper-ated by collectors' clubs and those of dealers who have mounted information areas as well as for-sale listings are becoming reliable sources of information on unusual items.

Variations

Impact on Value: Moderate

Production variations are fairly common, and usually do not increase or decrease value. Occasionally, however, variations that resulted from experimentation, though not widely collected, will command higher prices than comparable normal examples. Such is the case with glaze variations in Steubenville's American Modern, for instance.

A variety of mixtures and firing techniques were tried by Iroquois in a search for the perfect glaze or shape. If you find a piece that features a "T" next to the Casual by Iroquois backstamp, you've found a collector's item—the experimental glaze or shape designation in this instance does make the piece more valuable.

Homer Laughlin's Brittany underwent mold changes at least three times in its long production run, but no one makes any distinction among the three shapes. Whether you have an early-style creamer—which is more rare—or a common second-style creamer, they're likely to be priced exactly the same.

- **Experimental ware.** While production variations are generally overlooked, experimental and prototype pieces are often given lots of attention. There are very few one-of-a-kind pieces of dinnerware. When companies tested pieces, they usually did so in batches to determine whether there would be manufacturing glitches, firing problems, and so on. Hundreds of experimental lines were never put into production, but pieces frequently escaped the plants by way of employees. Most experts don't like to put prices on experimental work, because there are so few reference points, and the market for them can be entirely unpredictable.

- **Factory flaws.** Bauer Pottery glazes are notoriously thin and bubbly. Collectors have come to accept that, and it hasn't decreased the value of collectible Bauer lines. Glaze pops, thin spots, drips, sand trapped under the glaze, and other factory flaws should be noted by sellers. The asking price may be the same as for an unflawed piece, so it's mainly a matter of the buyer's taste whether factory flaws make a difference in value or appeal.

This Tamac of Oklahoma pitcher shows a glaze skip on the handle, a factory flaw that may or may not affect value, depending on the collector's preferences. *Photo courtesy of Retrospective Modern Design.*

Anomalies—cup handles unevenly applied, or a glaze that doesn't cover the whole piece—are trickier to evaluate. Most collectors don't want "seconds," but some appreciate these manufacturing defects as part of the process of making pottery. Whether such anomalies make a piece more valuable is again in the eye of the beholder.

Attribution
Impact on Value: High
The big names in pottery, whether companies or designers, will always be in demand. Ask seasoned collectors and dealers if they've ever heard of the Colonial China Company or West End Pottery and most will say no. Then ask if they've heard of companies in operation at the same time, making similar products, such as Homer Laughlin, Knowles, Hall, and Harker—and you'll get a resounding yes.

Similarly, if a designer is widely recognized—Raymond Loewy or Rockwell Kent, for instance—collectors will avidly seek any and all of their creations. Sascha Brastoff was a premier designer of California pottery in the 1950s. His hand-signed pieces (signed "Sascha Brastoff," not "Sasha B," a signature used by his decorators) are real prizes for discriminating collectors. A large charger plate by him (16" or more in diameter) books for $1,500. Yet, if a

This 1970s-era Happy Face mug is a nice example of McCoy's novelty-pattern dinnerware. (This short line also included a cookie jar.) The mugs spawned import look-alikes, but you can always tell "the real McCoy" because they are marked and are a little bigger and a lot heavier than the wannabes. *Photo courtesy of Home Grown Antiques.*

designer's name is not as immediately recognized, even if the work is first-rate—such as that of Mary Grant for Franciscan or Elliott House for Vernon Kilns—the signature or attribution will have no or low impact on market value.

Reissues, Reproductions, and Fakes

Reproductions and fakes do not pose the problem to dinnerware collectors that they do to collectors in other categories. No one is producing knockoff lines intended to deceive the unsuspecting. However, so many companies produced so many shapes and decorations that a similar line may be confused with—or pawned off as—a more expensive line by an uninformed or unscrupulous seller.

Novices may look at a line of solid-color dinnerware and be quick to call it a Fiesta knockoff. But remember that Fiesta was not the first or only line of colorware. Stangl and Bauer were actually the first to use bold colored glazes.

Exceptions to the Rule

While dinnerware as a category has not generally been plagued by reproductions or fakes, some trendy specialties have experienced problems. Cookie-jar collectors know that they must always be on the lookout for reproductions, fakes, and fantasy pieces.

One well-known example of a repro that wrought havoc in the marketplace is the Little Red Riding Hood cookie jar. Originally made by Regal China and distributed by Hull, it was copied by a Mexican manufacturer. Unfortunately, the fakes are reasonably good; however, they are smaller in both diameter and height, so the experienced collector can tell the difference.

Unscrupulous sellers occasionally "make what was old new again," for example by refiring old Shawnee cookie jars and adding decals and gold trim to increase value. Not only do these forgeries look like the originals—they are the originals!

The best defense against all fakes is an educated, discerning eye. Also, collectors' clubs will alert members when fraudulent copies show up in the marketplace.

As a rule, vintage American dinnerware does not command prices high enough to entice contemporary manufacturers, such as some Asian companies which have made an industry of cheap reproductions of antiques, to try to pass off new dinnerware as old. However, there are a few exceptions (see box above). Nobody has the exclusive right to produce rose-decal dinnerware or solid-color dinnerware. There have been instances when a company made a product so similar to one currently in production that legal action was taken. One such case was in the mid-1990s, when the discount chain Target commissioned a Chinese company to make a line called Cantinaware to be sold at its stores in the United States. The colors were similar to Fiesta's and, more important, so was the design. The Homer Laughlin China Company took Target to court, and the final ruling was that Cantinaware had to be removed from the market.

Companies sometimes use the same decals made famous by other potteries. The patterns imitated include Bakerite's Silhouette; Hall's Autumn Leaf, Red Poppy, Orange Poppy, and Crocus; and Universal Potteries' Cattail. The decals are applied to

93

shapes not used in the '30s or '40s, and the new pieces are marked, so there should be no confusion between old and new.

Manufacturer reissues are usually undertaken with the designer's approval. For instance, Eva Zeisel authorized reissues of some of her designs in recent years. Reissues are uncommon, and the manufacturer's motive in making one is usually to "feed the fire," or encourage collectors and increase the market value of dinnerware overall. More people than ever appreciate both the old and new versions.

The Business of Collecting

There are some keys to protecting your collection which will pay dividends many times over. Unless you amass a huge, museum-quality dinnerware collection, the record-keeping and insurance chores won't take much of your time.

Save your receipts. One good idea is to staple the dealer's business card to the receipt. For online purchases, save all e-mail between yourself and the seller. It is difficult to get a receipt from many businesses on the Web, so it's doubly important to save credit-card bills, e-mail, and any other documents pertaining to the sale. This practice additionally enables you to keep track of sellers you may want to contact again in search of a similar piece.

Making an Inventory

Keeping an inventory should be simple. If you want to use your computer, there are a number of software programs available for inventory management.

If you prefer a handwritten record, make up a simple form that describes the piece, the person you bought it from (name, address, phone number, and e-mail), the price you paid (as well as the price asked, if you wish), where and when you bought it, and the specifics of its condition and any flaws. Make photocopies or printouts of the blank form and then get into the habit of filling one out for each addition to your collection.

Photographic or video records of your collection are great idea, whether or not your insurer requires them. You should store your inventory, in whatever medium you've chosen, in a secure, fireproof place—a home safe or a safe-deposit box, if you have one.

Surf Ballet by Sascha Brastoff, pattern introduced in 1954. *Photo courtesy of Retrospective Modern Design.*

Getting an Appraisal

An official appraisal is a thoroughly researched, written, and certified evaluation of an item or a collection. It must include the reason for the appraisal (different reasons will result in different values); a complete description of the items, including photos; the method of research used; the resources consulted; the method of valuation used; and the market for which the items are being evaluated. An appraisal is a legal document, requiring considerable time and research, and will be expensive—often amounting to more than the value of your collection.

Not many collectors invest in an appraisal just to satisfy their curiosity or ascertain that their dinnerware is appreciating satisfactorily. An appraisal may be warranted if you want to insure an extremely valuable collection or donate it to a charity or museum and receive a tax write-off, or if you're involved in a divorce settlement or other lawsuit. For ordinary purposes, such as establishing value for shipper reimbursement of an item broken in transit—a local antiques dealer or even an authoritative book price is usually sufficient.

Before committing to an appraisal, find out how the appraiser will determine your fee. Be wary of any appraiser who bases it on the value of your item or collection. Most will charge you an hourly rate plus any expenses incurred in researching information specific to your collection. Remember that an ethical appraiser will take pains to remain disinterested—never offering to buy an item he or she appraised, for example.

Insuring a Collection

Modest dinnerware collections will usually be covered by your homeowner's policy as ordinary household contents. Consult your agent to find out if you have adequate coverage. If you decide to attach a rider to your homeowner's policy, be sure any rare and/or expensive pieces are documented and listed individually.

There are companies that specialize in collectibles insurance, and several authorities recommend these low-cost policies as the best choice. Also, you'll find that some collectors' clubs and associations offer group rates—another benefit of joining.

This Oriental-motif plate is an example of the interesting restaurant ware available to the alert collector. Made by the Technical Porcelain and Chinaware Co. (TEPCO), located in El Cerrito, California, from 1922 until the 1970s, this pattern was probably sold to one or more Chinese restaurants on the West Coast. TEPCO is noted almost exclusively for its restaurant and hotel ware. *Photo courtesy of Home Grown Antiques.*

eBay is the Best "Appraiser" Money Can't Buy

A writer researching a collectors' guide had six Fiesta 9" plates with a turkey decal. He checked several price guides, where they were valued at $95 to $105 each. When he finished photographing the plates for his book, he decided to sell them on eBay. He put one plate, in perfect condition, up for auction with a reserve price of $75. There were no bids. Another seller was auctioning a plate identical to his except for the color of the band around the plate. The starting bid amount was $50, but there were no bidders.

When it was time to price the turkey plates for his book, the author decided to put one up with an opening bid of $9.99 and no reserve. It sold for $54—half its book price! Over the next few months, he auctioned the others with the same opening minimum, closing at different times of day and on different days of the week. The final results were the same in each case: $50 to $55. The writer used this range as the book price in his new guide.

Under some circumstances you'll need a professional appraisal. But if an informal "appraisal" is enough, search completed online auctions, carefully taking into consideration the condition of the pieces, and you'll get accurate values without spending a penny.

Red Wing's Village Green, represented here by a salt-and-pepper set, was one of the most successful lines from the 1950s. It was introduced in 1953 and continued for about a decade. *Photo courtesy of Home Grown Antiques.*

Lazy Daisy creamer, milk pitcher, and cup, from the Informal line designed by Ben Seibel for Iroquois, pattern introduced in 1958. *Photo courtesy of Retrospective Modern Design.*

LIVING WITH YOUR COLLECTION

Setting your table with period dishes can provide you with personal enjoyment and satisfaction several times a day. And it can speak volumes about your sense of design style and creativity.

Perhaps you keep several sets at hand—one for everyday use, another for small gatherings of friends and family for informal meals. Then you have the grand set that comes out for holidays and major entertaining events. Of course, there's always the set you've just started to build, and the ones you keep safely packed until you decide you need a change. Once you're hooked on dinnerware collecting there's really nothing to stop you from going on and on with it!

Your changes of tabletop are sure to be noticed and appreciated as expressions of your flair for creating special occasions, large and small. They tell people that you appreciate fine design, and that you're not timid about making a statement. Some may see your dinnerware collecting as an aesthetic or historical interest on your part—there's likely to be an intriguing story that goes with these unusual dishes. And when you're not using your dinnerware collection on the table, it provides striking focal points of color, shape, and pattern in decorating almost every part of your home.

Displaying Your Collection

Most collectors start by filling china cabinets and corner cup-boards with their precious acquisitions, but quickly run out of space. They soon take to the walls, and fill every available space in the kitchen and dining room. That's when it hits them: Why stop there? You can enjoy your dishes in any room of the house you please!

Furniture and built-in cabinets. China cabinets, hutches, sideboards, and other display furniture often have plate rails or grooves cut into their shelves to accommodate vertical display of saucers, plates, and platters. A curio cabinet is perfect for a collection of demitasse cups or salt-and-pepper sets. Use a small chunk of museum wax or clay (available at glass and china boutiques) to ensure that pieces stay put if the piece of furniture is accidentally bumped.

Stands. Plate stands in appropriate sizes provide a secure way to display plates, saucers, platters, and chargers. You can find stands made of wood, acrylic, or metal, and some will accommodate more than one piece.

Wire hangers. Spring-tension wire plate hangers are intended for wall display and will keep your plates secure. Limit wall displays to pieces you don't use on the table often, because mounting and removing the hanger repeatedly can scratch the edges of the plate or mar any rim decoration. And if a plate hanger needs to be straightened, take it off and reattach it—sliding the hanger over the plate will scratch your plate. Be sure to use picture hooks of sufficient strength to hang your plates.

Cup hooks. Space cup hooks far enough apart to avoid cups' knocking together.

Nesting. Plates and bowls, or cups and saucers, may be nested to show them in ersatz place settings. But be careful not to stack more than two or three high, to avoid easily tipped displays.

Wall shelves. Mounting shelves on the wall is an excellent way to showcase a dinnerware collection in any room—but it's best not to put dishes directly above the stove, where they're likely to accumulate a combination of grease and dirt that's difficult to remove. Running shelves high on the wall minimizes the risk of accident, but be certain all shelves are mounted on studs and are strong enough to hold the weight they will have to bear.

You may want to consider having your kitchen cabinets re-fronted with glass to show off your dinnerware. You can even have low-voltage lighting installed inside the cabinets to put your dishes on display while keeping them away from dust and airborne grease.

Don't create a permanent dinnerware display in a location that's exposed to direct sunlight for prolonged periods. Strong sun can fade hand-painted designs, compromise the integrity of the clay body, catalyze crazing, and weaken decals or metallic decoration. Decaled dishes should also be protected from prolonged exposure to artificial light, which will eventually cause the designs to fade.

Clever collectors think of many original ways to display their dinnerware: plates and bowls used as incense holders, Zen gardens, jewelry boxes, or coin-and-trinket holders. One collector uses a Vernon Modern California sugar bowl without its lid to show off a collection of baby spoons. Express your sense of self and style.

Harlequin eggcup and individual creamer by Homer Laughlin, pattern introduced in 1938. An inexpensive alternative to Fiesta, Harlequin was sold exclusively through Woolworth stores. *Photo courtesy of Retrospective Modern Design.*

If you are tempted to use hollowware pieces like tureens to display plants, be sure you use a nonporous liner inside, to prevent minerals from staining your dinnerware. Even so, this is a risky practice for any piece you really value. It's best to look for a flawed or slightly damaged example of the piece to use as a decorative item.

Save Those Pieces

The thought of a broken dish makes most collectors cringe. But save those broken pieces and start a new collection. When you have enough, they can be set into grout to make a beautiful mosaic backsplash for your kitchen or bathroom, or added to fresh cement for garden stepping-stones. One collector designs her own flowerpots using shards because she likes the creative flair the bright, beautiful pieces add to her home.

Carrera Modern gravy with underplate by Iroquois. *Photo courtesy of Retrospective Modern Design.*

Storage and Protection

If you store dishes for extended periods, avoid extremes of heat and cold, as well as moisture. While some pottery is unaffected by dramatic shifts in temperature, extreme heat or cold may cause crazing in pottery that's susceptible to this condition. Pottery will eventually absorb moisture and, while mold and mildew probably won't hurt a piece in perfect condition, if there is crazing or a tiny chip, spores will get under the glaze and ruin the pottery.

Never wrap your dishes in newspapers—ink will stain them, especially if they're light in color, and may never come off entirely. Unused newsprint is great, however. Check with your local newspaper to see if they give away (or sell cheaply) the roll ends. You can also buy bolts of newsprint affordably from moving-supply companies. Otherwise, use tissue paper or bubble wrap.

As long as they'll be stored in a dry environment, cardboard boxes are suitable—but don't overload them. Plastic storage containers, available at home centers and housewares stores, are a better bet. They're strong, easily stacked, and will keep their contents dry and safe.

In general, dinnerware is too bulky and not conspicuously valuable enough to be a target for thieves. Not long ago, a collector who has about two thousand pieces of Fiesta and more than one thousand examples of Universal Potteries' Oxfordware—all openly displayed—suffered a break-in and robbery at his home.

You guessed it: the thieves took the VCR, television, and CD player, but his prized pottery collection was left untouched. There's little chance that someone will break into your house to steal your Franciscan dishes. But if you have a $50,000 cookie-jar collection, you may need to invest in a security system (indeed, your insurer may require it).

Care and Cleaning

Most collectors cherish their dinnerware and don't consign it to the dishwasher. Even recent wares marked "dishwasher safe" are at risk—more from harsh dishwasher detergents than from the dishwasher itself. Over time, the chemicals in detergents will dull the glaze's luster and fade the decals. A set of dishes can go from "like new" to "worn out" in a few short years.

All the safe cleaning supplies you'll need are already in your kitchen or bathroom. The one you should never use, however, is household bleach. Here are some tried-and-true remedies.

Grease buildup. Dinnerware displayed on open shelves, especially in the kitchen, may accumulate a stubborn layer of grease. Use a dishwashing liquid specifically formulated to dissolve grease. Soak the dishes in water to which some dishwashing liquid has been added, then dip an old, soft toothbrush in undiluted dishwashing liquid and scrub to remove any remaining spots.

Glue residue. Stickers, labels, and masking tape often leave a sticky residue that's hard to remove. Put a small amount of nail-polish remover on a cotton ball; test first on an inconspicuous spot if the glue to be removed is on the face of the dish.

Tea stains. A teapot or cups with stubborn tea stains may be treated by pouring boiling vinegar into the stained ware. Allow the vinegar to soak for several minutes, then add a little salt and ice. Swirl this solution around inside the stained item.

Rub marks. Grayish rub marks commonly seen on dinnerware that may originate from contact with some metals, such as aluminum, or even from rubbing against other dishes, can be removed with silver polish.

Stains. Stains of unknown origin can sometimes be removed by overnight soaking in a solution of water and baking soda or a solution of water and 3 percent hydrogen peroxide. If your dinnerware has any kind of metallic trim or overpainting, don't try these remedies.

Mineral deposits. Often difficult (if not impossible) to remove, calcium residue and hard-water marks can sometimes be improved by soaking in an extra-strength denture cleaner. Try scrubbing with full-strength cleaner on an old, soft toothbrush if soaking doesn't work.

TM

COLLECTOR'S COMPASS
Dinnerware Don'ts
- Don't use bleach or products containing bleach.
- Don't use steel wool or abrasive cleansers.
- Don't use peroxide on pieces with metallic or colored trims applied over the glaze.
- Don't try to repair crazing by "melting" the glaze in a kiln or extremely hot oven.

Repairs and Restoration

If a rare or valuable item sustains significant damage, the only way to salvage any value is to take it to a professional who specializes in dinnerware restoration. Even if you spend big bucks, the market value of the repaired item will be greatly diminished. Still, it's often worthwhile to save an object to which you're sentimentally attached or one that is the centerpiece of your collection.

Unless you are in a large urban center, you'll probably need to locate a restoration specialist through your collectors' club or a

Leaching Lead and "Radioactive Red"

Much of the dinnerware produced before the 1970s was made with glazes that contain lead. (All U.S. potteries were required to stop using lead in glazes in 1972.) So long as the glaze on your vintage dinnerware is intact, there is no danger from lead poisoning—despite the scare stories. Dishes imported from Italy and Mexico pose more risk than pre-1972 dinnerware made by American potteries. Avoid using vintage dinnerware when the glaze is compromised—including crazing—and never heat an acidic food or liquid, such as tomato sauce, lemon juice, or vinegar, on vintage ware in a microwave or conventional oven. You should also avoid storing an acidic food or liquid in a vintage vessel.

Red glazes (what most people would call orange, not a true red) contain traces of uranium oxide. But scientific research has determined that there is no risk in eating from these dishes—again, so long as the glaze is not impaired and you do not heat or store an acidic food on them.

Fiesta teapot in red. In 1943, Fiesta red was discontinued when the war limited the supply of uranium oxide, which was used to produce the glaze. When Homer Laughlin was able to obtain depleted uranium oxide in 1959, the popular red made a return and remained in production through 1969.

local antiques dealer. Some businesses advertise in trade publications and even exhibit at pottery and dinnerware shows, where a specialist sometimes repairs items on site.

Amateur repairs render any piece of dinnerware worthless in a monetary sense. However, if you like the piece and would miss it—but it isn't worth the cost of professional repair—you can glue it back together yourself, using any suitable glue from the craft store. If you glue an item, don't use it thereafter for food service. There are also products that work as fillers for chips and cracks, and paints for touch-ups.

IF AND WHEN YOU DECIDE TO SELL

As great as your passion for dinnerware is, you may someday need or want to sell some or all of your collection. If so, there are a variety of ways to go about it. Some are quicker than others, some involve more work for you, and some are likelier to be more profitable.

One of the most common reasons to sell is to trade up or concentrate on more valuable examples. Or you may have acquired duplicates in the course of buying large lots for the sake of the few items you needed. Also, personal circumstances change. You may have a major expense to finance, or perhaps you're downsizing your household and simply don't have the space for your huge collection.

You may have been collecting dinnerware all along with the hope that you'd buy well and be able to turn a nice profit. If you're a speculative collector, timing your sale to catch the market at its peak is a matter of close attention, research, and luck!

Whatever your reason for selling, and whether you're selling a few pieces or a whole collection, here's where good record keeping pays off. If you have described every item in a database or on a set of inventory forms, it will be easy to review your collection and decide what you want to sell. And if you took care to capture the details of each item's condition and defects when you bought it, you're already a long way toward writing a listing—for an ad, a price tag, or an online auction.

Selling through a Dealer

You Want to Trade Up or Sell a Few Duplicates

What do you do with the pieces you've outgrown? The next time you go to a pottery-and-dinnerware show—or a general antiques show—try taking a couple of pieces along to see if you can find a dealer who will buy or trade. If you have a rare item, it's probably better to try to sell it, but if a dealer has what you want, he or she may be willing to trade.

You Want to Sell Your Entire Collection

Selling your entire collection to a dealer will net you the lowest return on money invested, because dealers pay a fraction of current market value—usually 50 percent or less. They have overhead and expenses, and have to make a profit to stay in business. But if you've held your dinnerware for a long time, even the wholesale prices a dealer will pay could give you a gain on your investment.

Depending on your circumstances, the speed and convenience of selling your collection as a whole may outweigh the money issue. You will avoid the headaches of keeping track of individual sales, packing, and shipping, not to mention bad checks, disgruntled purchasers, and being stuck with items that won't move.

You'd Like to Consign with a Dealer

You may make a greater profit by consigning with a dealer, but it will probably take longer to sell your collection. If you go this route, you must have an item-by-item inventory and establish a price for each piece, or a single price for the whole set. Discuss your expectations with the dealer—he or she will be reluctant to accept your collection if you have unrealistic expectations that will keep the items in inventory too long. Pay close attention to clarifying the details of your agreement, which should be written down and signed by both of you.

One of the best reasons to enter into this type of arrangement is that full-time dealers cover more ground than you can—

simultaneously operating at shows, in malls, on the Internet, and running advertisements. They also have more contacts and a ready supply of want lists from other collectors. The commission you pay for access to the dealer's network is well worth it.

Syracuse China restaurant mug with Sundown cowboy design. Syracuse got its start in 1841 in Syracuse, New York, under the name Empire Pottery. In 1971 the company discontinued its lines for the home and concentrated entirely on its commercial lines, becoming one of the top producers of hotel and restaurant ware. Institutional ware, made of vitrified china, is much sturdier than pottery for the home. *Photo courtesy of Home Grown Antiques.*

Selling Your Collection Yourself

Selling your collection yourself is the most time-consuming and labor-intensive option, but should net you the most profit. Not only will you need to be on top of the market, you must also present the dishes for sale, establish a network of contacts, and—if you're selling by mail order or online—follow through on every transaction. Remember, you'll be on the other side of customer-service issues and hassles—bad checks, complaints, tracking shipments.

The Internet is the most popular venue for selling dinnerware on your own. On the plus side, you're placing your offerings before an enormous audience. And if you have a valuable or rare item, it takes only two people desperate to add that item to their collections to drive the bidding higher than what you could hope to realize from other sources.

But there are drawbacks: if you use one of the big auction

sites, like eBay, Amazon, or Yahoo, and you make an innocent mistake or fail to hold up your end of a transaction, you may receive negative feedback that will make other buyers wary of you. You must register to sell (fees will be automatically billed to your credit-card account), pay listing fees, and take care of all the bookkeeping. In addition, you must write good descriptions, answer questions, and follow through with shipping and other details of each sale. There's no guarantee that your items will sell, and unless you set reserve prices there's a risk that they may sell for much less than you're expecting.

Another way to sell a collection yourself is to advertise in trade papers, newsletters, or magazines that specialize in dinnerware. You'll be spending money with no guarantee of results.

A downside to online auctions and mail-order sales is that you have to wait for your money. And do wait for your money! Specify in all ads that personal checks must clear before you'll ship merchandise. PayPal, BillPoint, or another credit-card payment service will allow immediate risk-free payment to you, but you'll have to set up an account and specify these payment services in your ads or listings.

When you're determining whether to sell your pieces singly or in groups, think about how you went about building your own collection. There are some collectors who will buy a complete, or, more often, a nearly complete set, to get started in a desired line or pattern. Others may be filling in missing pieces or concentrating on getting the serving pieces and accessories. Others may be eyeing your ad as a way to replace a single broken piece in an otherwise complete set. There's no magic to listing your items one way or another, but recognize that you may be appealing to different collector interests depending on how you offer them.

The All-Important Description

An honest, complete, and enticing description is essential to a successful sale. If you're auctioning wares online, a good digital photograph is necessary as well. Interested buyers scan dozens of listings and click through them quickly. If your description doesn't catch their eye, or if it raises more questions than it answers, they're likely to move on. Or you may be barraged with phone calls and e-mail questions. It's better to spend a little more time composing your original copy.

Provide an accurate accounting of flaws, repairs, and damage. That doesn't mean you can't write an attractive ad, extolling the attributes of your merchandise, but there's no point in subterfuge. If the item doesn't match your description, the purchaser will quite correctly demand a refund of the purchase price, postage, and any insurance he or she paid.

Here's an example of a poorly worded listing in an online auction:

> Russel Wright dinner plate, 10", manufactured by Steubenville. Vivid salmon, one of the most searched-for colors. Great addition to your vintage collection! Be sure to check my other Russel Wright auctions this week. Winning bidder pays shipping. I accept PayPal for your convenience. Thanks for bidding.

What's wrong with this ad? There is no "salmon" color—the correct identification is coral, and it is not a highly sought color. There is no mention of condition, and the pattern isn't stated. Why would you want to visit the seller's other auctions when she has done no research and isn't knowledgeable about her merchandise?

Now here's an ad written by a seller who not only knows exactly what he's selling but tried to anticipate questions a potential buyer might have:

> Four mottled terra cotta dinner plates, Raymor Modern Stoneware by Roseville, designed by Ben Seibel. The mottling on these 10" plates is stunning (see photo). There is a ⅟₁₆" chip on the underside of the rim, not visible from the top, on one plate. A second plate has a tight hairline crack, about ¾" long, at the rim. The set is otherwise in excellent condition and, even with these minor imperfections, it is an outstanding addition to any collection. If yours is the winning bid, these plates will be carefully wrapped, double boxed, and sent via UPS. Due to the heavy weight of the plates, shipping charges inside the U.S. will be $17.50; others, please inquire. Pay by money order or PayPal and receive immediate shipment. Thanks for bidding, and good luck!

RESOURCES TO FURTHER YOUR COLLECTING

Shows

The All-American All-Pottery Show and Sale
Copper Hill School
900 Everitts Road
Flemington, NJ 08822
Telephone: 908-782-9631
Run by the Stangl/Fulper Collectors' Club, this show claims to have "the best, the rarest, the most beautiful, interesting and collectible examples of American pottery, dinnerware and ceramics from the mid-19th century to 1980."

American Pottery, Earthenware and China (APEC) Show and Sale
Illinois State Fairgrounds
Springfield, IL
Contact: Norman Haas, organizer
264 Clizbe Road
Quincy, MI 49082
Telephone: 517-639-8537
Annual September event featuring American dinnerware and pottery.

Atlantique City
P.O. Box 1800
Ocean City, NJ 08226
Contact: Brimfield Associates
Telephone: 800-526-2724 *or* 609-926-1800
E-mail: info@atlantiquecity.com
Web site: www.atlantiquecity.com
Billed as the "largest indoor art, antique and collectibles fair in the world," with more than sixteen hundred booths on ten acres.

Brimfield Antique Shows
Route 20
Brimfield, MA 01010
E-mail: lmyers@tiac.net
Contact: Quaboag Valley Chamber of Commerce
Telephone: 413-283-2418
Web site: www.brimfield.com
One of the largest and best-known antiques shows in the United States. A town of three thousand grows to

more than thirty-five thousand on show days in May, July, and September. More than five thousand dealers participate. This show is not a controlled event and has no central governing body.

Eastern States China, American Pottery, and Dinnerware Exhibition (ESCAPADE)
St. Laurence Parish Center
Laurence Parkway
Laurence Harbor, NJ
Contact: P.O. Box 9
Metuchen, NJ 08840
Telephone: 732-738-5677
Features dealers from seven states selling American-made pottery, china, and dinnerware of the twentieth century. Held in November each year.

East Liverpool Pottery Collectors' Convention
Contact: East Liverpool Chamber of Commerce
529 Market Street
East Liverpool, OH 43920
Telephone: 330-385-0845
Fax: 330-385-0581
E-mail: tourism@elchamber.com
Web site: www.elchamber.com
An annual convention, usually held in mid-June.

Farmington Antiques Weekend
Farmington, Connecticut
Contact: P.O. Box 580
Fisher, IN 46038
Telephone: 317-598-0012
Fax: 508-839-4635
E-mail: JonJIndpls@aol.com
Web site: www.farmington-antiques.com
One of the big shows, with more than six hundred dealers. Second weekend in

June and Labor Day weekend. "Farmington is a show where you can shop and buy with confidence. Our dealers have pledged to have no reproductions or new merchandise, no crafts or dried flowers."

The Hall Haul
Web site: www.geocities.com/~peachie0607/hallevents.htm
An annual convention for Hall collectors. This witty Web site is maintained by a Hall enthusiast who advertises Hall events, links to other sites of interest to Hall collectors, and showcases her items for sale as well as other personal-interest pages.

The Los Angeles Pottery Show
Contact: P.O. Box 726
Highland, CA 92346
Telephone/fax: 909-864-1304
E-mail: LApotteryshow@aol.com
Web site: www.lapotteryshow.com
Both art pottery and dinnerware designers and manufacturers are represented.

Manhattan Antiques and Collectibles Triple Pier Expo
Piers 88, 90, and 92
New York, NY
Contact: Stella Show Management Co.
147 West 24th Street
New York, NY 10011
Telephone: 212-255-0020
Fax: 212-255-0002
E-mail: Jstella327@aol.com
Web site: www.stellashows.com
Held during two weekends in March and two in November, the expo features six hundred exhibitors.

**Modern Times 20th Century
Design Show and Sale**
Glendale Civic Auditorium
1401 Verdugo Road
Glendale, CA 91205
Contact: Modern Times
P.O. Box 342
Topanga, CA 90290
Telephone: 310-455-2894

Dealers Specializing in Dinnerware

All Wright
Carmen Brady and Pierre Allaud
E-mail: russel@all-wright.com
Web site: www.all-wright.com
Web site specializing in Wright's modern
design, especially strong on
dinnerware, including some rare
Bauer Pottery pieces designed by
Wright's wife, Mary Wright.

Atomic Scott
Scott Vermillion
819 West Buena Ave.
Chicago, IL 60613
Telephone: 773-871-7068
E-mail: atomicscot@aol.com

The Bauer Boys
Greg McDermott, Joel Patrick Rose, and
Daniel Ryan
Telephone: 760-327-2717
E-mail: gmcd@bauerboys.com
Web site: www.bauerboys.com
Specialists in Bauer; you'll see a remarkable
assortment of Ringware in particular,
including rare pieces. This site also
sells rare Bauer books and other
highly collectible dinnerware such
as Eva Zeisel's Town and Country,
Franciscan Starburst, and more.

Dining Elegance
P.O. Box 4203
St. Louis, MO 63163
Telephone: 314-865-1408
E-mail: info@diningelegance.com
Web site: www.diningelegance.com

E-dish
815 East 2100 South
Salt Lake City, UT 84106
Telephone: 801-486-8282 *or* 888-767-8282
Fax: 801-485-7644
E-mail: slc@edish.com
Web site: www.edish.com

Fiesta Plus
Mick Chase and Lorna Chase
380 Hawkins Crawford Road
Cookeville, TN 38501
Telephone: 931-372-8333
E-mail: fiestaplus@yahoo.com
Web site: www.fiestaplus.com
Fiesta Plus has a long history of selling in
Tennessee and is now on the Internet
as well. You can find examples of
most important modern American
dinnerware.

Home Grown Antiques
Michele Miele and Frank Miele
7 First Avenue East
Kalispell, MT 59901
Telephone: 406-756-7259
Web site: www.homegrownantiques.com
American dishes are the specialty, with a
wide selection of Metlox, Franciscan,
Homer Laughlin, Russel Wright,
Bauer, Royal, and other popular
American manufacturers. This business
started online but has since expanded
to include a retail store.

Retrospective Modern Design
P.O. Box 305
Manning, IA 51455
Telephone: 888-301-6829 (toll free)
    or 712-653-3678
Fax: 712-653-3027
E-mail: modern@hialoha.net *or*
    wiese@pionet.net
Web site: www.retrospective.net
Carries an extensive selection of the most
    popular mid-century dinnerware
    designs by Metlox, Eva Zeisel, Russel
    Wright, and Ben Siebel, among
    others. Emphasis on high-quality
    merchandise and customer service.

Robbins Nest Antiques
Darryl Robbins
124 Forrester Road
Glasgow, KY 42141
Telephone: 270-678-3661
Web site: www.robbinsnest.com
One of the best Web sites specializing in
    Homer Laughlin china; features a
    large pattern library to help people
    find replacements. Also offers a
    variety of other dinnerware.

Twentieth Century Designs
Jim Medeiros
P.O. Box 3386
Fayville, MA 01745-0386
Telephone: 508-370-7330
Fax: 240-220-7224
E-mail: jim@fiestajim.com
Web sites: www.FiestaJim.com *and*
    www.TwentiethCenturyDesigns.com
Despite the nickname, Fiesta Jim has a little
    of everything in twentieth-century
    collectibles, including lots of
    dinnerware in patterns by Homer
    Laughlin and other potteries.
    Medeiros sells online and at shows,
    including Brimfield.

Auctions

Internetauctionlist.com lists some of the
top live auctions across the country. Check
the antiques categories for appropriate
listings, with locations, dates, and times.

Treadway Gallery
2029 Madison Road
Cincinnati, OH 45208
Telephone: 513-321-6724
Fax: 513-871-7722
E-mail: info@treadwaygallery.com
Web site: www.treadwaygallery.com

Verlangieri Gallery
P.O. Box 844
Cambria, CA 93428-0844
Telephone: 805-927-4428
Fax: 805-924-0110
E-mail: verlangieri@thegrid.net
Web site: www.calpots.com
Michael Verlangieri is an important dealer
    in California pottery who conducts
    two online auctions each year of
    Bauer, Sascha Brastoff, Franciscan,
    Pacific, Metlox, and much more.

Publications

The Antique Trader Weekly
P.O. Box 1050
100 Bryant Street
Dubuque, IA 52004-1050
Telephone: 800-334-7165
Web sites: www.csmonline.com/
    antiquetrader *and* www.collect.com/
    antiquetrader

Ceramics Monthly
P.O. Box 6102
735 Ceramic Place
Westerville, OH 43086-6102
Telephone: 614-523-1660
Fax: 614-891-8960
Web site: www.ceramicsmonthly.org

The Daze

P.O. Box 58
Clio, MI 48420
Telephone: 810-670-3293
Fax: 810-670-3294
E-mail: dgdaze@aol.com
Web site: www.dgdaze.com
Articles and sale listings; covers tableware
of all types, including American
dinnerware.

Echoes

P.O. Box 155
Cummaquid, MA 02637
Telephone: 800-695-5768 *or*
508-362-3822
Fax: 508-362-6670
E-mail: hey@deco-echoes.com
Web site: www.deco-echoes.com
Focuses on classic and modern design,
including dinnerware.

Pottery Collectors' Express

P.O. Box 221
Mayview, MO 64071-0221
Telephone: 816-584-6309

Pottery Lovers Newsletter

Pat Sallaz
4969 Hudson Drive
Stow, OH 44224
E-mail: Newsletter@potterylovers.org

Set Your Table

P.O. Box 22481
Lincoln, NE 68542-2481
Telephone: 800-600-2127
Telephone/fax: 402-423-4865
E-mail: sranta@setyourtable.com
Web site: www.setyourtable.com
Annual directory of antiques dealers,
matching services, and others who
specialize in locating, selling, and
restoring discontinued or hard-to-find
patterns of dinnerware, flatware,
hollowware, and glassware.

Collectors' Clubs and Associations

Fiesta Collector's Club

P.O. Box 471
Valley City, OH 44280
Web site: www.chinaspecialties.com
Publishes a quarterly newsletter. Limited-
edition Fiesta designs are produced
exclusively for members.

Franciscan Collectors' Club

8400 Fifth Avenue NE #5
Seattle, WA 98115
E-mail: gmcb@ix.netcom.com
Web site: www.gmcb.com/franciscan

Frankoma Family Collectors Association

P.O. Box 32571
Oklahoma City, OK 73123-0771
Web site: www.frankoma.org
A nonprofit organization dedicated to the
promotion of Frankoma pottery as a
collectible. Membership includes the
quarterly journal *Pot and Puma* and
the quarterly *Prairie Green Sheet*—
dedicated to buying, selling, and
trading Frankoma. Annual national
convention.

Hall China Collectors Club

P.O. Box 360488
Cleveland, OH 44136
Web site: www.inter-services.com/
HallChina

Homer Laughlin China Collectors Association

P.O. Box 26021
Crystal City, VA 22215-6021
Telephone: 877-874-5222
Web site: www.hlcca.org

**International Association of
Dinnerware Matchers**
P.O. Box 656
High Ridge, MO 63049-0656
Web site: www.iadm.com
Organization dedicated to helping
customers locate hard-to-find pieces
of china, crystal, and flatware from
about 1900 to the present.

Red Wing Collectors Society
P.O. Box 50
Red Wing, MN 55066
Telephone: 651-388-4004 *or* 800-977-7927
E-mail: rwcs1@win.bright.net
Web site: www.redwingcollectors.org
Six newsletters per year, and a national
convention.

Stangl/Fulper Collectors Club
P.O. Box 538
Flemington, NJ 08822
Telephone: 908-782-9631
Web site: www.stanglfulper.com
National organization dedicated to the
collecting of Stangl and Fulper
pottery; publishes a quarterly
newsletter; sponsors annually an
auction in June and a pottery show
in October.

Eva Zeisel Collectors' Club
22781 Flamingo Street
Woodland Hills, CA 91364
Telephone: 818-222-1367
E-mail: patmoore@evazeisel.org
Web site: www.evazeisel.org
Formed in 1999, the club already has a
valuable Web site devoted to this
important twentieth-century
dinnerware designer. Quarterly
newsletters and a complete catalog
of Zeisel's work from the 1920s to
the present are planned.

Online Auction Sites

www.ebay.com—The granddaddy of the
e-auction houses, and undoubtedly
the best. All other sites pale in
comparison when you're searching
for dinnerware.

http://auctions.yahoo.com—This is a
good site for buyers, with a fairly
large inventory but not much action
among bidders. That means sellers
generally keep asking prices low, and
you may pick up surprising bargains.

www.potteryauction.com—There's no fee
for buyers or sellers on this site, but
there isn't a great deal of inventory
either. You may pick up a bargain,
or you may get bored and leave.

It's worthwhile to take a look at other
online auction sites, too. Many come and
go quickly, but some of the promising
entries for dinnerware at the time this book
went to press are:
    www.auctionaddict.com
    www.auctionport.com
    www.auctions.excite.com
    www.boxlot.com
    www.liveauctiononline.com
    www.modernauction.com
    www.UBid.com

E-groups

Bauer Pottery
www.bauerpottery.com
Bills itself as "a Collectors Homepage for
the J. A. Bauer Pottery Company
1885–1962." You can find a useful
gallery of photos, representative
samples of the Bauer lines, a message
board, and other information.

Fiesta

www.vincel.com/wwwboard

Discussion group for Fiesta and other vintage Homer Laughlin wares.

Ohio River Valley Pottery

www.ohioriverpottery.com/bbs

Emphasis on Homer Laughlin, Knowles, Taylor Smith and Taylor, and other Ohio River Valley potteries, but includes general information on American dinnerware as well.

Retrospection

www.egroups.com/subscribe/retrospection

An e-mail list for anyone interested in mid-century modern American dinnerware.

Wing Tips

www.RedWingNet.com

This site is committed to antique Red Wing artware, dinnerware, and stoneware. There is a history section, a marketplace, and a popular feature called "Ask Wally and Paul about Red Wing."

Russel Wright

http://listserv.aol.com/archives/ russel-wright.html

Discussion list for anyone interested in the history or collectibility of Russel Wright designs.

Museums, Factory Tours, and Historic Sites

Frankoma Pottery

P.O. Box 789

2400 Frankoma Road

Sapulpa, OK 74067

Telephone: 918-224-5511 *or* 800-331-3650

Fax: 918-227-3117

E-mail: info@shopfrankoma.com

Web site: www.frankoma.com

Hall China Company and the Hall Closet (retail outlet)

No. 1 Anna Street (on Route 39)

East Liverpool, OH 43920

Telephone: 800-445-4255

Fax: 800-837-4950

E-mail: custserv@hallchina.com

Web site: www.hallchina.com

Self-guided tours of factory on weekdays; closed weekends.

The Homer Laughlin China Company

Sixth and Harrison Streets

Newell, WV 26050

Telephone: 800-452-4462

Fax: 304-387-0593

E-mail: hlc@hlchina.com

Web site: www.hlchina.com

Factory tours conducted on weekdays, but *reservations are required.* An excellent online tour can be found at www.fiestapottery.com.

Manitoga: The Russel Wright Center

584 Route 9D

P.O. Box 249

Garrison, NY 10524

Telephone: 914-424-3812

Fax: 914-424-4043

E-mail: info@manitoga.org

Web site: www.manitoga.org

The ecologically designed landscape and education center at Wright's home. Memberships available at various prices. Manitoga has annual collectors' events, educational seminars, and a newsletter.

The Metropolitan Museum of Art

1000 Fifth Avenue at 82nd Street

New York, NY 10028-0198

Telephone: 212-535-7710

Web site: www.metmuseum.org

Locate pottery and dinnerware in the American Modern exhibits.

Museum of Ceramics
400 East Fifth Avenue
East Liverpool, OH 43920
Telephone: 330-386-6001 *or*
    800-600-7180
Web site: www.ohiohistory.org/
    places/ceramics
Exhibits focus on the early years of pottery
    and dinnerware manufacture in the
    Ohio River Valley, especially the East
    Liverpool area.

Museum of Modern Art
11 West 53rd Street
New York, NY 10019
Telephone: 212-708-9400
Web site: www.moma.org

Replacements, Ltd.
1089 Knox Road
P.O. Box 26029
Dept. W7
Greensboro, NC 27420
Telephone: 336-697-3000 *or*
    800-737-5223
Fax: 336-697-3100
E-mail: inquire@replacements.com
Web site: www.replacements.com
The museum is home to more than two
    thousand rare and unusual pieces.
    The showroom and museum are
    open weekdays. Collectors interested
    in modern dinnerware and design
    will want to consult the museum
    exhibit calendar in *Echoes* magazine
    (*see* "Publications," above).

**Schein-Joseph International Museum of
Ceramic Art
New York State College of Ceramics at
Alfred University**
Alfred, NY 14802
Telephone: 607-871-2421
Web site: www.ceramicsmuseum.alfred.edu
New York State College of Ceramics is
    based at Alfred University, and this
    museum and teaching center houses
    more than eight thousand examples
    of ceramic art, from antiquities to the
    leading-edge artisans of today.

Libraries

Smithsonian Institution Libraries
Special Collections Department
NMAH 1041
Washington, DC 20560-0672
Telephone: 202-357-1568
Fax: 202-633-9102
E-mail: libmail@sil.si.edu
Web site: www.sil.si.edu/newstart.htm

Syracuse University Library
Department of Special Collections
Bird Library, Room 600
Syracuse, NY 13244-2010
Telephone: 315-443-2697
Fax: 315-443-2671
E-mail: arentsl@library.syr.edu
Web sites: www.syracuse.edu *and*
    libwww.syr.edu/information/
    spcollections/index.html

Thomas J. Watson Library
Metropolitan Museum of Art
1000 Fifth Avenue at 82nd Street
New York, NY 10028-0198
Telephone: 212-650-2225
Fax: 212-570-3847
E-mail: watson.library@metmuseum.org
Web site: www.metmuseum.org/
    education/er_lib.asp#tho
You must present qualified credentials to
    use the library on site, and an
    appointment must be made in
    advance. You can search the library
    catalog online at
    www.library.metmuseum.org.

Repair and Restoration Specialists

www.antiquerestorers.com
Search this general Web site for the
    porcelain/ceramics category to find
    an international listing of restorers,
    plus a state-by-state guide to restorers
    in the U.S.

Association of Restorers
8 Medford Place
New Hartford, NY 13413
Telephone: 315-733-1952 *and*
    800-260-1829
Fax: 315-724-7231
E-mail: andrea_restore@msn.com
Web site: www.assoc-restorers.com
Helps collectors locate a reputable
    restoration specialist in any
    geographical area.

Chips and Pieces
1310 Utica Street
Denver, CO 80204
Telephone: 303-623-4217
E-mail: aswilen@yahoo.com

Give Me a Break China
P.O. Box 5553
Napa, CA 94581
Telephone: 707-226-2924

Hamlin's Porcelain Restoration
14630 Manchester Road
Ballwin, MO 63011
Telephone: 636-256-8579

Mark's China-Pottery
101 West Olive Avenue
Fresno, CA 93728-3035
Telephone: 209-485-1998

Tindell's Restoration School and Studios
DiAnna E. Tindell
825 Sandburg Place
Nashville, TN 37214
Telephone: 615-885-1029
Fax: 615-391-0712
E-mail: tinrestore@aol.com
Besides restoration services, offers courses
    in restoration.

REPRESENTATIVE VALUE GUIDE

This guide is a price sampling of various shapes, patterns, and colors from particular potteries. For each pottery, we priced a dinner plate as a point of comparison. Rare serving and specialty pieces are also featured to show the upper end of the ranges. For the purposes of this guide, consider all items to be in very good to excellent condition. Names by which patterns are popularly known—if not their official names—are in quotation marks.

ITEM	SIZE	SHAPE/PATTERN/COLOR	DESIGNER	VALUE
BAUER (J. A. BAUER POTTERY COMPANY)				
Dinner plate	9"	Ringware/Chinese yellow		$34–$40
#12 mixing bowl		Ringware/orange-red		$130–$145
Salad bowl	14"	Ringware/Chinese yellow		$185–$225
32-ounce pitcher		Gloss Pastel Kitchenware	Murray	$50–$60
Cup & saucer		Monterey/burgundy		$25–$30
2-cup teapot		Monterey Moderne/chartreuse		$45–$50
Cereal bowl		La Linda/gloss green		$22–$25
FRANKOMA POTTERY				
Dinner plate	10"	Wagon Wheel		$15–$20
Trivet	6"	Lazybones		$50–$60
Chip & dip bowl	9"	Plainsman		$25–$30
Mini pitcher		Mayan-Aztec (Ada clay)		$40–$45
GLADDING McBEAN AND COMPANY/FRANCISCAN				
Dinner plate	10¾"	Starburst	James	$18–$22
Buffet plate	11¼"	Sea Sculptures, "Nautilus"		$22–$25
Salad plate	8"	Wildflower (hand-painted)		$34–$38
Salt & pepper		Apple (hand-painted)		$25–$29
Salad bowl	11"	Autumn		$45–$52
HALL CHINA COMPANY				
Dinner plate	9"	Autumn Leaf		$18–$20
Aladdin teapot		Autumn Leaf		$60–$65
Dinner plate	9"	Orange Poppy		$15–$18
Teapot		Donut shape/cobalt		$350+
Platter	17"	Tomorrow's Classic/Bouquet	Zeisel	$75–$85
HARKER POTTERY				
Dinner plate	10¼"	Royal Gadroon "Ivy Vine"		$10–$12
Cup & saucer		White Clover	Wright	$15–$20
Rolling pin		Hot-Oven, "Amy"		$125–$150
Teapot		Cameo, White Rose		$65–$75
HOMER LAUGHLIN CHINA COMPANY				
Dinner plate	10"	Fiesta/red	Rhead	$37–$40
Disk jug		Fiesta/medium green	Rhead	$1,000+
Dinner plate	10"	Harlequin/burgundy	Rhead	$23–$25
Dinner plate	10"	Virginia Rose/"Moss Rose" decal	Rhead	$12–$15
IROQUOIS CHINA COMPANY				
Dinner plate	10½"	Informal/"Harvest Time"	Seibel	$10–$12
Mug original style		Casual/white	Wright	$150–$200
Stacking salt & pepper		Casual	Wright	$25–$30
Fruit compote	5¼"	Impromptu/"Stellar"	Seibel	$25–$30

ITEM	SIZE	SHAPE/PATTERN/COLOR	DESIGNER	VALUE
METLOX POTTERIES				
Dinner plate	10"	California Aztec	Allen & Shaw	$23–$26
Teapot		California Provincial	Allen & Shaw	$135–$155
Cup & saucer		Central Park	Allen & Shaw	$14–$17
Salad fork & spoon		Sculptured Grape	Allen & Shaw	$65–$70
PFALTZGRAFF POTTERY COMPANY				
Dinner plate	10"	Country-Time	Seibel	$12–$15
Dinner plate	10"	Yorktowne	Mountain	$8–$10
40-ounce jug		Yorktowne	Mountain	$27–$30
RED WING POTTERIES				
Dinner plate	10½"	Town & Country/bronze	Zeisel	$40–$45
Quail shakers, pr.		Bob White		$45–$50
Creamer & sugar with lid		Lexington Rose		$30–$35
ROSEVILLE POTTERY COMPANY				
Dinner plate	10"	Raymor/autumn brown	Seibel	$20–$22
Sugar		Raymor/beach gray	Seibel	$25–$28
Teapot		Raymor/avocado green	Seibel	$150–$160
SOUTHERN POTTERIES (BLUE RIDGE)				
Dinner plate	10½"	Any hand-painted floral		$20–$25
Plate	9¼"	Any hand-painted floral		$12–$15
Chocolate pot		French peasant		$350–$400
Creamer & sugar with lid		Skyline shape		$25–$30
STANGL POTTERY				
Dinner plate	10"	Thistle		$15–$18
13-ounce coffee mug		Town & Country/brown		$25–$30
Soup/cereal bowl	5¾"	Town & Country/blue		$30–$35
B & B plate	6"	Golden Harvest		$5–$6
STEUBENVILLE POTTERY COMPANY				
Dinner plate	10"	American Modern*	Wright	$14–$16
Cup & saucer		American Modern**	Wright	$14–$16
Water pitcher		American Modern***	Wright	$75–$85
Nesting coffee pot		Contempora/mist gray	Seibel	$550–$650
Creamer		Contempora/charcoal	Seibel	$14–$16
*Granite gray **Chartreuse ***Coral				
TAYLOR SMITH AND TAYLOR CHINA COMPANY				
Dinner plate	10"	Lu-Ray Pastels/surf green	Thorley	$18–$20
Dinner plate	10"	Lu-Ray Pastels/Chatham gray	Thorley	$55–$60
Juice pitcher		Lu-Ray Pastels/Windsor blue	Thorley	$150–$160
Dinner plate	10"	Pebbleford/teal	Gilkes	$8–$10
Dinner plate	10"	Vistosa/cobalt	Thorley	$28–$30
VERNON KILNS				
Dinner plate	10"	Organdie		$12–$14
Drip-cut syrup		Organdie		$50–$60
Butter dish		Tickled Pink	House	$53–$60
Demi cup & saucer		Ultra California/buttercup	Turnbull & Bennison	$27–$30

a.d. Abbreviation for "after dinner," used to describe a small coffeepot, cup, saucer, creamer, or sugar bowl. *See* demitasse.

b and b Abbreviation for "bread and butter," a plate usually about 6" in diameter, depending on maker. Also known as a dessert plate or sherbet plate.

baker An oval serving dish, often used as a vegetable bowl. Some, marked "oven-safe," can be used as casseroles.

bisque Pottery that has been fired but not decorated or glazed.

blank Molded or cast pottery, bisque-fired but undecorated and unglazed.

casting A production method involving pouring clay into a mold to harden. Pieces formed by casting will usually have seam lines.

ceramic Any product (as earthenware, porcelain, or brick) made essentially from a nonmetallic mineral (as clay) by firing at a high temperature.

china *See* porcelain.

chop plate An oversize round serving plate, usually 12" or more in diameter.

cold paint Decoration applied over the glaze.

coupe Style of plate or bowl that has no rim.

crazing Fine cracks in the glaze of pottery. Usually caused by the expansion and contraction of the clay body and the glaze at uneven rates. Exposure to high heat can also cause crazing.

decal A film transfer decoration often used on dinnerware. Some decaled patterns have the appearance of hand painting.

demitasse or demi From the French for "half cup." This term usually describes small after-dinner coffee or tea services. Also called *children's dishes*.

dinner plate The standard plate for dinner service, usually measuring from 9½" to 10½" in diameter.

earthenware Pottery made from clays found close to the surface of the earth and fired at low temperatures—below 1150°C. Earthenware is opaque and porous (which is apparent when the glaze is broken and the clay absorbs the colors of food or liquids as stains). Historically, the vast majority of the world's pottery is earthenware, including about 95 percent of pottery produced today. Almost all collectible American dinnerware is earthenware.

finial Ornament or knob on a lid, usually elaborate in style.

flatware Pieces of dinnerware that are more or less flat, such as plates, platters, and chop plates. *Compare* hollowware.

glaze A mixture mostly of oxides (from alumina to zinc) applied to the surface of ceramic wares before final firing to form a moisture-impervious, glasslike finish that is both practical and decorative. A huge variety of minerals are combined in various glaze recipes to achieve certain colors and lusters. Hand-painted, filigreed, or decaled dinnerware is glazed and fired over the decorations. Metallic trim is applied after glazing and final firing.

hollowware Vessels (such as fruit dishes and soup bowls to pitchers, coffeepots, and casseroles) that have a significant depth and volume. *Compare* flatware.

institutional ware   Heavier ware, often porcelain, sturdier than standard dinnerware, made for restaurants, hotels, cruise ships, etc. Designs were often made especially for particular hotels and railroads.

ironstone   A heavy, durable institutional white pottery that gains its strength from the use of ground stone in the clay body. Devoloped in England early in the nineteenth century and employed typically for utilitarian purposes.

jiggering   A production method used in casting in which a machine forces clay to take on a specific shape.

luncheon plate   The standard plate for lunch or salad service, usually measuring from 8½" to 9½" in diameter.

mark   The signature of a pottery company on a piece of dinnerware—sometimes incised or impressed, most commonly stamped. Typically found on dinner plates, less frequently on serving pieces, but sometimes on all pieces of a pattern.

marriage   Describes the joining of two otherwise unrelated pieces of pottery, such as a casserole body and a lid. Married pieces are conspicuous if their shapes, colors, and patterns do not match, but more subtle if one or more of these elements appears to match.

porcelain   A hard, fine-grained, nonporous, and usually white ceramic ware made from a fabricated body of white-firing clays, feldspar, and quartz, and fired at high temperatures—1250 to 1400°C. When fired properly, porcelain approaches total vitrification, giving it its valued translucent quality.

redware   Earthenware pottery made of clay containing considerable iron oxide, especially that produced from the seventeenth through the nineteenth centuries from red clays naturally occurring in America in the East and Midwest.

restyling   Changing the design of a pattern after its introduction, a common practice for many dinnerware manufacturers. Fiesta is noted for this, as are most of the patterns designed by Russel Wright. Sometimes the original style is more valued, sometimes the restyled piece, depending on how quickly in the production run the change was made and how successful it was.

sagger   A case made of fireclay into which ceramic pieces are fitted to protect them during firing. Sagger marks are typically three unglazed areas on the bottom of the piece, where it was attached to the sagger.

stoneware   Pottery made from clays occurring in strata below topsoils, fired at temperatures between 1150 and 1300°C. Hard, durable, almost impervious to liquids, and with high thermal resistance, stoneware is used for ovenware and utilitarian wares.

transfer printing   A technique for decorating pottery invented in 1756, used most famously by potteries in Staffordshire, England, but also by many American potteries. A design is etched into a copper or other metal plate. The plate is inked and a tissue paper is applied. The inked design is then transferred on the tissue paper to the body of a bisque-fired ceramic piece, which is then glazed and fired again. This method of decoration typically leaves a "seam" where the print overlaps imperfectly. One famous transfer-printed pattern is Blue Willow.

whiteware   The body typically used in modern dinnerware, whether earthenware or porcelain. It first became popular among American manufacturers around the 1870s.

yellowware   Earthenware pottery made from buff clay and covered with a yellow transparent clay, popular for utilitarian dishes in the nineteenth century.

REFERENCES AND
SUGGESTED READING

Bagdade, Susan, and Al Bagdade. *Warman's American Pottery and Porcelain.* Iola, Wis.: Krause, 2000.

Chipman, Jack. *Collector's Encyclopedia of Bauer Pottery.* Paducah, Ky.: Collector Books, 1998.

Cunningham, Jo. *The Collector's Encyclopedia of American Dinnerware.* Paducah, Ky.: Collector Books, 1998.

————. *Homer Laughlin: A Giant Among Dishes,* 1873-1939. Gas City, Pa.: Schiffer, 1998.

Duke, Harvey. *The Official Price Guide to Pottery and Porcelain.* 9th ed. New York: House of Collectibles, forthcoming (2001).

Gibbs, Carl Jr. *Collector's Encyclopedia of Metlox Potteries.* Paducah, Ky.: Collector Books, 1995.

Gonzalez, Mark. *Collecting Fiesta, Lu-Ray and Other Colorware.* Gas City, Ind.: L-W Book Sales, 2000.

Huxford, Bob, and Sharon Huxford. *Collector's Encyclopedia of Fiesta: Plus Harlequin, Riviera, and Kitchen Kraft.* 9th ed. Paducah, Ky.: Collector Books, 2000.

Keller, Joe, and David Ross. *Russel Wright: Dinnerware, Pottery and More.* Malvern, Pa.: Schiffer, 2000.

Kerr, Ann. *Collector's Encyclopedia of Russel Wright.* Paducah, Ky.: Collector Books, 1997.

Lehner, Lois. *Lehner's Encyclopedia of U.S. Marks on Pottery, Porcelain and Clay.* Paducah, Ky.: Collector Books, 1988.

Levin, Elaine. *The History of American Ceramics: 1607 to the Present (From Pipkens and Bean Pots to Contemporary Forms).* New York: Harry N. Abrams, 1998.

Meehan, Kathy, and Bill Meehan. *Collector's Guide to Lu-Ray Pastels.* Paducah, Ky.: Collector Books, 1998.

Page, Bob, and Dale Frederiksen. *Franciscan: An American Dinnerware Tradition.* Greensboro, N.C.: Replacements, 2001.

Reiss, Ray. *Red Wing Dinnerware: Price and Identification Guide.* Chicago: Property Publishing, 1997.

Runge, Robert Jr. *Collector's Encyclopedia of Stangl Dinnerware.* Paducah, Ky.: Collector Books, 2000.

Snyder, Jeffery B. *Franciscan Dining Services.* Malvern, Pa.: Schiffer, 1996.

Whitmyer, Margaret, and Kenn Whitmyer. *Collector's Encyclopedia of Hall China.* 4th ed. Paducah, Ky.: Collector Books, forthcoming (2001).

ABOUT THE INTERNATIONAL SOCIETY OF APPRAISERS

The Collector's Compass series is endorsed by the International Society of Appraisers, one of North America's leading nonprofit associations of professionally educated and certified personal-property appraisers. Members of the ISA include many of the industry's most respected independent appraisers, auctioneers, and dealers. ISA appraisers specialize in more than two hundred areas of expertise in four main specialty pathways: antiques and residential contents, fine art, gems and jewelry, and machinery and equipment.

Established in 1979 and consisting of more than 1,375 members, the ISA is founded on two core principles: to educate its members through a wide range of continuing education and training opportunities, and to promote and maintain the highest ethical and professional standards in the field of appraisals.

Education through the ISA

In conjunction with the University of Maryland University College, the ISA offers a series of post-secondary professional courses in appraisal studies, including a two-level certification program.

The ISA recognizes three membership levels within its organization—Associate Member, Accredited Member, and Certified Member—with educational programs in place for achieving higher distinctions within the society. ISA members who complete the required coursework are recognized with the title of Certified Appraiser of Personal Property (CAPP). Through its pioneering education programs, the ISA plays a vital role in producing qualified appraisers with a professional education in appraisal theory, principles, procedures, ethics, and law as it pertains to personal-property appraisal.

Professional Standards of the ISA

The ISA is dedicated to the highest ethical standards of conduct, ensuring public confidence in the ability and qualifications of its members. To help members perform their work with the most up-to-date knowledge of professional standards, the ISA is continually updating, expanding, and improving its courses and criteria of conduct.

For more information about the International Society of Appraisers, contact its corporate offices:

Toll-free: 800-472-4732
E-mail: ISAHQ@isa-appraisers.org
Web site: www.isa-appraisers.org

ABOUT THE CONTRIBUTORS

Kathryn Wiese Gibson and her mother (and collecting mentor), **Jean Wiese,** have an insatiable desire for American dinnerware. In an effort to support their habit, this dynamic dinnerware duo started a replacement-dinnerware business four years ago, Retrospective Modern Design, which sells American dinnerware on the Internet and by appointment. While the particular passion of the mother-daughter team is mid-century modern, they also offer an array of more traditional dinnerware designs.

They have exhibited at regional and nationals shows, and Kathryn is a regular contributor to *Set Your Table* and other collecting publications.

You can reach them through their Web site, at www.retrospective. net; at P.O. Box 305, Manning, IA 51455; and toll-free at 888-301-6829.

Mark Gonzalez was born in East Liverpool, Ohio—known today as the pottery capital of the world. His grandparents worked at area potteries such as Homer Laughlin, Taylor Smith and Taylor, and W. S. George from the 1930s to the 1950s, and he himself has been collecting solid-color dinnerware such as Fiesta and Lu-Ray Pastels since 1981. He is the author of two books, *Collecting Fiesta, Lu-Ray and Other Colorware* (Gas City, Ind.: L-W Book Sales, 2000) and *An Overview of Homer Laughlin Dinnerware* (forthcoming, 2001), and maintains a Web site (www. ohioriverpottery.com) devoted to the identification of shapes, treatments, and marks found on American dinnerware.

Frank Miele and his wife, **Michele Miele,** are the owners of Home Grown Antiques. They have been selling on the Internet at www. homegrownantiques.com for the past five years, and Michele recently opened an antiques store in Kalispell, Montana. They specialize in American dinnerware of the twentieth century, such as Homer Laughlin, Bauer, Frankoma, Metlox, and Russel Wright, and carry other American pottery and glassware.

The Mieles have a son, Carmen, and a daughter, Meredith, who are being groomed to join the family business.

Christopher J. Kuppig has spent his entire career in book publishing. For several years he directed programs at Dell Publishing, Consumer Reports Books, and most recently Chilton Book Company—where his assignments included managing the Wallace-Homestead and Warman's lines of antiques-and-collectibles guides.

In 1997, Mr. Kuppig founded Stone Studio Publishing Services, a general management consultancy to book publishers. Acting as series editor for the Collector's Compass series has given him the opportunity to draw upon his wide-ranging network of contacts in the collecting field.

Mr. Kuppig resides with his wife and three children in eastern Massachusetts.